Seasons of Savannah

Produced in cooperation with

COMMUNITY COMMUNICATIONS, INC.

Contributing writers

TOM COFFEY

MARGARET W. DEBOLT

LORRAINE JOHNSON-COLEMAN

BRET LOTT

Seasons of Savannah

Photography

THE SAVANNAH COLLEGE OF ART AND DESIGN

Corporate profiles

GEORGIA R. BYRD

The Savannah College of Art and Design and Community Communications, Inc., would like to express our gratitude to the following companies for their leadership in the development of this book.

BRASSELER USA®

CHATHAM COUNTY GEORGIA 1777

CITY OF SAVANNAH GEORGIA

VADEN

DARBY BANK & TRUST COMPANY

Georgia Ports Authority

GEORGIA SOUTHERN UNIVERSITY

Robin Fowler

Great Dane Trailers

Gulfstream
A GENERAL DYNAMICS COMPANY

H.O. SYSTEMS

SAVANNAH AREA CHAMBER

Seasons of Savannah

With essays by Tom Coffey, Margaret W. DeBolt,
Lorraine Johnson-Coleman and Bret Lott

Corporate profiles by Georgia Byrd
Cover photograph by Lynn Wright

Featuring photography by students of the
Savannah College of Art and Design

COMMUNITY COMMUNICATIONS, INC.
Publisher: Ronald P. Beers

STAFF

Acquisitions: Henry S. Beers
Publisher's Sales Associate: Mel Merk
Editor in Chief: Wendi L. Lewis
Profile Editor: Mary Catherine Richardson
Editorial Assistant: Heather Ann Edwards
Savannah Editors: Cameron Spencer, Betsy Brairton
Photo Captions: Jeff Eley
Design Directors: Janice Shay, Scott Phillips
Designers: Janice Shay, Winslett Long
Photo Editor: Jenny Kuhla
Contract Manager: Christi Stevens
National Sales Manager: Ronald P. Beers
Sales Assistant: Sandra Akers
Acquisitions Coordinator: Angela P. White
Accounting Services: Stephanie Perez
Print Production Manager: Jarrod Stiff
Pre-Press and Separations: Artcraft Graphic Productions

CCI

COMMUNITY COMMUNICATIONS, INC.
Montgomery, Alabama

David M. Williamson, Chief Executive Officer
Ronald P. Beers, President
W. David Brown, Chief Operating Officer

Printed in USA
First Edition 00-011358
Library of Congress Catalog Number: 00-011358
ISBN: 1-58192-031-8

Chia Chong

Table of CONTENTS

VAUG
THE SPIRIT SHALL RETURN UNTO

Introduction

Cities change with the seasons. In winter, New York dons a cold, gray haze; smiles are concealed by thick woolens for months. Chicago's icy winds turn to a toasty passion in summer, demanding two distinct wardrobes that vary from closet to attic. Atlantans savor the orange, red and golden hues that the north Georgia trees show off in the fall, and spring there is best signaled by the crack of a bat.

But only in Savannah can one sit on a porch swing and nap in November, tend a garden in January, and lie on a blanket surrounded by a fragrant floral display in March. The beauty of Savannah, Hostess City of the South, is truly without season.

The shiny gold dome of City Hall presides over the buildings along River Street and symbolizes the strength of Savannah's past, a carefully preserved history that has blended seamlessly with contemporary comforts. America's first planned city encompasses a 2.5 square mile historic district—one of the largest urban historic districts in the country—accentuated with ornate ironworks and the architectural brilliance of an old European town. This small-town setting allows one to walk from a historic house museum or business to lunch at a sidewalk café, and horse-drawn carriages, trolleys, and pedicabs abound to take the visitor to any downtown destination.

Located in the semi-tropical deep South, this Low Country city enjoys lush foliage and diverse wildlife. Renowned for its National Historic Landmark District, its live-oak-lined avenues and more than 200 parks and recreational facilities, Savannah welcomes the visitor to explore relics of historic Fort Pulaski or Old Fort Jackson, view a working steam engine in an old railroad roundhouse, or take advantage of the seven fishing piers, nine public boat ramps, nine tennis courts, and five public golf courses. Add to these a world-class weightlifting facility and a new swimming complex, and one can appreciate why Savannah has become desirable both as a place to live and as a tourist destination.

Savannah is well-known for her spirit of celebration, too. The Sidewalk Arts Festival, Savannah Shakespeare Festival, and Savannah Film and Video

Festival draw large crowds, as do the Savannah Onstage International Arts and Savannah Jazz festivals. Another eagerly anticipated event is Savannah's famous St. Patrick's Day celebration. More than 600,000 parade watchers and participants come to Savannah to join in the music, dancing, and cultural displays that mark the second largest Irish gathering in the country.

Maggie Van Wie

Galleries abound in response to the large artists' community spawned by the Savannah College of Art and Design. While galleries and boutiques are patronized by day, the evening belongs to Savannah's eclectic restaurants, enticing thousands with culinary delights that range from elegant to down-home. Whether traditional Low Country fare, New Southern cuisine, or any number of multicultural and ethnic choices, Savannah's dining establishments offer savory meals for tourist and local alike.

After dinner, Savannah's balmy evenings offer romantic walks along cobblestoned streets as well as live entertainment—from jazz and piano bars to the Savannah Symphony, from blues and rock concerts to country music and dancing.

Photography students at the Savannah College of Art and Design devoted a year to capturing the spirit of the Hostess City—her history, leisure activities, celebrations, and diverse cultural pursuits—in *Seasons of Savannah,* a collection of photographic essays depicting the seasons. The sections are introduced by thoughts on the season penned by four nationally recognized local writers. The result is a visual treasure, inviting the reader to discover the pleasure of exploring Savannah and, ultimately, to come enjoy her in person.

What Makes a Leader?

The dictionary defines leadership as a "foremost position"—the first, the head of the class. A leader commands, a leader influences, guides, conducts, escorts; a leader sets a precedent.

Within a community, leaders are those who are unafraid to step up to meet the challenges of today, and who have the foresight to plan for the needs of tomorrow. These are the visionaries, the individuals or groups that boldly take the next step, encouraging those around, "Come on! This way! Join me and see how much we can grow with each other's help!"

Perhaps nowhere is leadership more vital in a community than in the development of its business sector. The lifeblood of any city is its business community. A healthy, thriving business and industry base ensures jobs for citizens, tax revenue necessary for maintaining public property, city services and roads, and a healthy economy overall—which, in turn, is good for businesses. Everybody benefits.

All members of a community feel the influence of business leadership. It is evident in corporate sponsorships benefiting education, the arts, and the environment. Leadership is visible in a ready population of volunteers who donate their time and talents to assist those less fortunate in their community, making for a richer quality of life for all citizens. And, leadership is the force that inspires one to dream, to reach a little higher, to try a little harder.

Leadership is the force that makes Savannah special.

Richard Rodriguez

Brasseler USA

Brasseler USA, an internationally known giant in the world of dental, medical, and industrial rotary cutting instruments, is headquartered in a modern facility located on the city's expanding southside. Its recently renovated facilities in Savannah employ more than 225 residents of Savannah and neighboring communities.

As the company continues to provide its customers with the highest level of satisfaction, Brasseler USA excels by providing the most innovative product design and development in the industry. The dental industry is growing and expected to double over the next several years and Brasseler USA is heavily involved in working with leading clinicians in order to remain an innovative solution provider.

The future looks very promising for Brasseler USA as Savannah's manufacturing and distribution facility continues to grow in order to meet the needs of the company and the markets it serves. Brasseler USA will continue to be a leader in its industry as well as the Savannah area.

Chatham County

From the picturesque seas of the Atlantic Ocean and its beautiful Tybee Island beaches to the pine forests of its western suburbs, Chatham County is a land rich in beauty, natural resources, and industrious leadership. With its courthouse standing tall in the midst of the downtown area and local government officials headquartered in an historic building on Wright Square, Chatham County continues to climb in the rankings as one of the southeast's fastest-growing areas for industry, recreation, and tourism.

Touting the country's largest historic district of 2.5 square miles, Chatham County continues to be the ideal setting for corporate meetings, vacationers, and retreats.

Indeed, Chatham County geography, lifestyle, and tradition make it the perfect oasis for vacationing or living. With Old World charm, high-tech abilities, and strong local leadership, it remains to be one of this country's most valued treasures.

Richard Rodriguez

The City of Savannah

From the 23-karat gold dome that crowns City Hall to the impressive cable-span bridge that links Savannah to South Carolina's shores, signs of thoughtful planning are evident throughout this picturesque city. Savannah's past has been delicately preserved and, along with careful planning, this city has become one of the country's most popular places to visit and live.

Seeking a place as an asylum for debtors, in 1733, British General James Oglethorpe staked his claim on a high bluff, naming it Savannah. Through the years, the city has maintained Oglethorpe's plan, preserving it through meticulous and constant care and judicious planning.

Today, Oglethorpe's bluff is filled with colorful pubs, shops, and restaurants. Across the waterfront, an enormous trade center casts an impressive reflection in the busy Savannah River, reminding Savannahians of all cultures that careful planning, combined with progressive leadership, lead to a city filled with prosperity.

Jessica Purvis

Dan Vaden Dealerships

At 73, Dan Vaden is a long way from retirement. His great love for the automobile business is evident in each of the dealerships he owns and operates.

As the Savannah area grew, so did Dan Vaden's business from one dealership to multiple franchises and locations. The Vaden Automotive Group includes Dan Vaden Chevrolet-Oldsmobile, Dan Vaden Chevy-Olds at Truckland, Vaden Nissan, Vaden Volkswagen, Vaden Hyundai, Vaden Isuzu, Vaden Suzuki, and Vaden Commercial Trucks in Savannah. He also has dealerships in Brunswick and Hinesville.

Dan Vaden has 50 years of experience in the automobile business, but he says that, "every day is a learning experience because no two cars and no two customers are alike." The Vaden Group started with one employee—Dan Vaden himself. Today, the organization employs about 350 people, including several family members.

Today, Vaden is focused on opportunities to grow the business and is optimistic about his future in automobiles. "I'm really just getting started," he said.

Darby Bank and Trust Company

In an age where big institutions are primarily banking on technology for success, a small-town bank is making big-city strides using a personal, friendly approach to business. Darby Bank and Trust was able to land Walter Bowden, a prominent and highly respected Savannahian whose passion was banking and whose affection has been small communities.

"Savannah was a logical expansion market for Darby Bank because of my contacts and the connections of our Board of Directors and the fact that Connie Williams, a daughter of the founder, lived there. We have made an effort to go out and initially do business with people that we know to get a good, solid base for business in place, without the risk of dealing with unknown quantities," said Bowden.

Competing with giants is no easy task, but, according to Bowden, Darby Bank's one-on-one approach to banking is the key to the bank's future.

Georgia Ports Authority

The Georgia Ports Authority's deepwater port facilities in Savannah and Brunswick represent two of the most dynamic transportation systems in the world—linking water, rail, and highway infrastructure to benefit businesses and residents throughout the state of Georgia.

The core business activity of the Georgia Ports Authority is facilitating international commerce to and from locations around the world. More than 80,000 jobs in Georgia are connected directly or indirectly to public and private port sector activities, thus making the Georgia Ports Authority one of the state's most efficient economic facilitators.

To remain competitive, the Georgia Ports Authority focuses on the diversity of the marketplace and serves the dynamic needs of international customers. The Authority is committed to keeping alive its commitments to the citizens of Georgia and Georgia businesses to develop strategies, nurture partnerships, and prepare port facilities that will propel the Port of Savannah into one of the most respected ports in the world.

Richard Rodriguez

Georgia Southern University

Georgia Southern is the largest and most comprehensive center of higher education in the southern half of Georgia and the third largest enrollment statewide, with 14,400 students. Georgia Southern is one of the top two universities of choice for new freshman, including HOPE scholars, and attracts students from every state and 80 nations.

Georgia Southern's hallmark is a superior undergraduate experience, emphasizing academic distinction, excellent teaching, and student success. The University's graduate programs are offered on campus, at satellite centers, and by distance and on-line delivery to expand advanced education and develop professional leadership in fields critical to regional development.

The 634-acre park-like campus offers a learning environment for students and the public enhanced by a museum of cultural and natural history, a botanical garden, and a unique wildlife education center. The University's Division I athletic teams compete in the Southern Conference, and have earned five national football championships since 1985.

GREAT DANE TRAILERS

When you pass a sleek and gleaming trailer on the road, chances are, the trailer and its mud flaps will bear the logo of Great Dane Trailers. The same ideals that created the company one hundred years ago are still evident in the company's modern facilities, but time and technology have enhanced Great Dane's products, making them the leader among long-lasting, better-built trailers. Today's trailers are the result of highly skilled engineers using space-age technology.

Two goals have driven the company—building superior products and fulfilling customer needs. The impressive facility is a typical phenomenon of the American economy—a small business that grew and changed as the country offered opportunity for profitable change. It has been the commitment to consistent quality and innovation that has indeed made Great Dane the industry leader. And it is these same principles that will drive Great Dane Trailers into the next century.

Gulfstream Aerospace Corporation

Much like its home city—historic Savannah—Gulfstream's milestones have filled the history books, and publications worldwide have illustrated the company's dominance in the global market of business jets.

The success of Gulfstream's current aircraft line has never been stronger. With more than a hundred Gulfstream V's in customer service, Gulfstream aircraft continue to be the world's best-selling large-cabin, long- and ultra-long-range business aircraft.

And while Savannah has celebrated the company's continued prosperity, across the globe, Gulfstream's dominance has soared with customers including countries such as Kuwait, Saudi Arabia, and Japan to name a few.

While the company remains an industry giant, it is also one of southeast Georgia's friendliest and most philanthropic employers as well as Chatham County's largest industrial employer. With a past so rich with achievements, the future of Gulfstream is secure as one of the most widely known and respected brands in the world.

Amanda Brandt

H.O. Systems

Amid the serene Savannah ambiance lies a fast-paced company that is becoming one of the nation's leading providers of billing and customer care business systems for wireless carriers. From its headquarters in a stately commerce building, H.O. Systems produces and supports mission-critical billing software to the telecommunications industry. With a mission statement declaring "Service Beyond Software," as its driving force, the company's position in the market is continuing to soar.

With a client coverage in most of the United States, H.O. Systems' impressive list of clientele has helped spread the word about the Savannah-based company's innovative products and services, keeping the company ahead of its competition.

With a bright future ahead, H.O. Systems' President S. Hart Williford attributed the past success of the company to its dedicated group of employees. "We have great people working here. We commit to hiring employees who are aggressive, with high energy and committed to quality—the ones who'll see us through in our fast-paced market place. For this we are truly proud."

Savannah Area Chamber of Commerce

America's first planned city, Savannah, Georgia, has relished her reputation as a lavishly dressed lady adorned in architectural brilliance and drenched in year-round blossoms. But with ingenious community leadership, she has aged with grace and energy to attract a new league of guests.

The city that once drew visitors to her shores to explore the gardens and homes of the nation's largest historic district is now appealing to the masses with a diverse menu of events, activities, and some of the country's most heralded restaurants.

Savannah is an easy sell. The sheer brilliance of its eclectic architecture, its mild climate, and its lush, tropical landscaping makes it the perfect year-round destination.

Whether it's the unique charm or a feature-length film that attracts the visitor to Savannah, it is the city's people who extend the warmth and grace of true Southern hospitality to its guests and keeps them coming back for more.

Richard Rodriguez

Spring

by TOM COFFEY

SPRING MAKES SAVANNAH LIVABLE. Not that it isn't already livable, or almost livable, or somewhat livable. Springtime, simply, *really* does the trick.

One must understand Savannah to fully appreciate how spring works here. You see, Savannah is seldom, if ever, really cold. Oh, a few winters ago the thermometer dropped to 13 degrees. And there might be a snowfall, lasting at least overnight and into the next day. But few Savannahians can remember a real winter.

In fact, former Mayor John Rousakis summed it up quite neatly one day at a City Council meeting, addressing a visiting delegation from England: "Savannah has nine cold days a year, and this just happens to be one of them. I apologize to you. Please stay a couple more days and see what I mean."

There might be an Irish influence on Savannah's springtime. Not every city in America celebrates St. Patrick's Day the way Savannah does. Some, in fact, don't celebrate at all. But Savannah does, and it always arrives three days before spring.

Now think about that for a moment. It's still winter when St. Patrick's Day arrives, but St. Patrick's Day is not intended for winter, especially in a town like Savannah, which has the second largest parade in the nation.

That parade simply has to have warm and springlike weather, and it gets it.

But then, our town really has two celebrations on St. Patrick's Day—one centered on the parade and the other centered on River Street and numerous topside places. Usually, the ones involved in the second celebration do not see the parade. They're too busy, mostly drinking and frolicking. It's amazing the way the separate festivities can go on at the same time, and one not interfere with the other.

But let's take spring after it really gets here. The vernal equinox comes on March 20, and with it comes many things, among them tourists. But remember this: Tourists are here long before spring. What spring does bring is *more* tourists.

Now there are some here who wish tourists would find another place to visit. These are, for the most part, the ones who have come here to retire. They'd simply like to live in peace. They wish John Berendt had never written *Midnight in the Garden of Good and Evil* (though it's a good bet that all of them have a copy), and of course they wish the tours would not be taking visitors all over downtown in slow-moving buses.

But the tourists overwhelm those who object. There are too many of them, and remember, too, that tourists spend a lot of money here. That's where the businesses come in. The businesses indeed are thankful for John Berendt, and though some of them criticize his book, they wouldn't trade Berendt and the heavy impact he has made upon Savannah for anything.

There is also SCAD, the acronym for Savannah College of Art and Design. Now SCAD fits into Savannah's spring very well. Not that it hasn't fit in before and after spring, but spring brings in enough warmth for the SCAD students to come out and draw their art on the sidewalks of Forsyth Park. It's more than just a few strokes. SCAD's Sidewalk Arts Festival is, indeed, ART—to the point where it becomes a shame that, as soon as the festival is over, the art must be cleaned off the sidewalks.

But more than SCAD or anything else, springtime in Savannah brings in such things as flowers in volumes, Savannah Shakespeare Festival, reopened pools, greenery, balmy weather, outdoor festivals, Memorial Day, tourists.... Spring makes Savannah *really* livable!

Richard Rodriguez

Spring comes early to Savannah, announced by azaleas, dogwoods, Carolina yellow jasmine, and Cherokee roses. Gardeners start preparing in January. During March, garden tours abound in the Historic District. A Savannah gardening rule: "Plant your nasturtiums before Washington's birthday and you won't be disappointed come Easter!"

Bailey Davidson

Robin Fowler

The 1996 Olympic yachting competition was hosted by Savannah and took place on Wassaw Sound. Recreational boating and sailing have always drawn people to these waters.

Robin Fowler

SCAD students literally paint the town with murals undertaken as class projects and as volunteers in the city-wide Public Mural Project.

The theme of the sea pervades the city. Even the county water treatment facility has been creatively camouflaged with aquatic allusions.

Bailey Davidson

Everyone gets into the game! From college athletics to minor leagues, from pro

Richard Rodriguez

teams to community sports, Savannah offers activities for players and fans alike.

Richard Rodriguez

Savannah has a long military history. Established as an outpost to buffer the wealthy planters in South Carolina from swashbuckling pirates and Spaniards colonizing Florida, the city also endured sieges and blockades throughout the American Revolution and the Civil War. Parades and reenactments are staged at several area venues throughout the year.

The architecture of Savannah is as varied as her citizens. Sometimes grand, sometimes magical, these buildings provide terrific opportunities for wonderful photography.

Yamacraw Bluff, the landing spot of Gen. James Oglethorpe's original settlement, later became the center of Savannah's cotton warehouses before the Civil War.

Across the river, development of a new hotel and trade center on Hutchinson Island complements the community and enhances a riverfront different from the one Oglethorpe knew.

Robin Fowler

James Albrecht

Private gardens are some of Savannah's best-kept secret places. A stroll down Jones Street provides delightful surprises.

Richard Rodriguez

Bailey Davidson

Savannah loves a parade and all the pomp and pageantry it might provide. The Savannah St. Patrick's Day Parade includes many guest celebrities. Swords and hats are optional.

Bailey Davidson

Bailey Davidson

Bailey Davidson

Richard Rodriguez

Richard Rodriguez

Everyone is Irish on St. Patrick's Day.
Erin go Bragh!

Richard Rodriguez

Richard Rodriguez

Isi Sarfati

Beginning with green eggs, flaming green grits and Irish coffee, the celebrations start early

Richard Rodriguez

Richard Rodriguez

Bailey Davidson

and continue long into the night. Savannah's historic district is awash in people wearing green!

Richard Rodriguez

Winslett Long

Savannah is synonymous with preservation—something is always being restored. The community takes great pride in preserving its significant historical structures, such as the Cathedral of St. John the Baptist.

Richard Rodriguez

The port of Savannah has welcomed visitors from around the world and boasts a multicultural population whose ancestors hail from all parts of the globe.

Spring festivals abound. One of these is the popular International Festival hosted by Savannah College of Art and Design students on Broughton Street in April.

Robin Fowler

Richard Rodriguez

LINK YOU ARE AN ANIMAL.
AMATEUR!
COLOR

At the annual Sidewalk Arts Festival, Forsyth Park's walkways are transformed into continual, colorful, transitory masterpieces. April showers soon wash them away!

Robin Fowler

Summer

by LORRAINE JOHNSON-COLEMAN

YOU KNOW, I think that if I were ever going
to do something really and truly brilliant,
Something so downright incredible that folks
would still be talking about it way after I die
When I'm buried six feet under
with my toes turned up toward the sky,
I think I would just have to wait until the long
days of summer have managed to pass themselves by
Because this is when this lady called Savannah is
at her absolute best
Breezing herself about in one long hot, smoldering sigh.

Yes, my girl is truly something else. Some would say that she
is perhaps the last grande dame in all of the South
But whether that is true or not, there is no question
that she deserves all of her praise and more;
For this Southern belle maintains her classic beauty
even when the humidity smothers and the temperature soars.
And of course this is that time of year when company loves to come calling—
all of those tourists tramping throughout this entire place
But she is ever the gracious hostess
ready with a comfortable place to stay, a home-cooked meal and
A welcoming smile spread charmingly across her face.

Oh, I do believe that it would be ever so easy
to get carried away while sitting comfortably underneath a great big shade tree just
Admiring Savannah's summer beauty of
sunlit mornings, afternoon warm showers,
That moss that dips seductively down from the trees
and of course the sparkling white sands of that beach called Tybee.
Glory, Savannah in summer is one magnificent place!
So I figure that if I have half a chance at coming
Up with something one day that is sure to be brilliant, guaranteed to beat all
Then maybe I ought to wait awhile,
Perhaps until that moment that the lady graciously retreats into fall.

Amanda Brandt

The beach on Tybee Island, just twenty minutes from downtown Savannah, is the perfect summer getaway.

Bailey Davidson

Richard Rodriguez

The recently restored Tybee Island Lighthouse and Museum

presides over a variety of summer activities—from kayaking and

Isi Sarfati

kite-flying, to creating sand sculptures on the nearby beach.

Isi Sarfati

Paul Baucomb

Jie Yu

Afternoon clouds in late June provide unexpected showers or inspire a daydream or two. What do you see?

Many of Savannah's late-nineteenth-century homes boast delightful detailing and decorative paint schemes accented here by the bright summer sunlight. Color is the rule—lots of it too!

Bailey Davidson

Amanda Brandt

Alongside trendy retail stores and coffee shops, longtime local merchants contribute to the delightful visual mix of downtown. There is something for everyone on Broughton Street!

Lynn Wright

Jonathan Slavkin

Savannah's year-round temperate climate supports subtropical plant life such as this beautiful palm frond.

Jason Meek

Come right in! Elegant parlors in the Historic District are perfect for afternoon tea and lemonade. Savannah relishes her reputation as the Hostess City of the South.

Bailey Davidson

Shrimp boats, shrimp bisque, shrimp salad, shrimp dip, boiled shrimp, fried shrimp,

Jessica Purvis

steamed shrimp, shrimp grits, shrimp creole, shrimp etouffé, shrimp scampi.

From Forsyth Park to City Hall, a stroll down Bull Street has it all: places of worship, historic homes, pubs, picturesque cafes, boutiques and galleries. Savannah is a place you can discover over and over again.

Robin Emery

Jen Buffett

Robin Emery

A Victorian District landmark, the "Gingerbread House" is a favorite location for weddings, receptions and other social celebrations.

In contrast to the architectural grandeur associated with Savannah's historic district, charming and unpretentious shops, confectioneries and other businesses also dot the area.

VAN'S BARBER SHOP
Van's Barber Shop
Barber Shop
NO SMOKING

The Original
SHABAZZ
World Famous
BEAN PIE
SHABAZZ

SAVANNAH CHECKER CLUB
MEMBERS ONLY

NITA'S
PLACE

Mark Uzmann

Fall

by **Bret Lott**

THEN ONE MORNING LIGHT FALLS DIFFERENTLY, and the gracious shadows we've known throughout this sun-drenched summer have taken on a sharper tongue, a little harsher hue, all without word to us save for the whisper somewhere inside us of the sun's agreement with itself: *I am leaving.*

On this morning, the soft shade the world has afforded all summer long has suddenly and slowly changed. With that change, the architecture of these homes on the square takes on a beguiling charm for the way darkness hides in new angles of shadow and light. There's an alluring mystery in the way doorways and windows and columns and eaves all take on the strange and bedeviling angle of time's passing with these new shadows, shadows all evidence of how this latest affable summer seemed to stop time altogether.

Now silver Spanish moss in the live oaks on the square seems more silver than ever in this bold new light, the moss a kind of silver that gently heralds our own age coming upon us; broken light through the boughs of these live oaks scatters across the square itself not the gentle and refined gems this same sun had let fall just yesterday morning, but soft-edged shards as keen and cutting as a genteel woman's cordial curse.

And here, this single bittersweet morning, is the mystery of autumn in Savannah, this single morning we move through different light amidst architecture cloaked in lingering darkness, one step made into these strengthened shadows while each moment the earth tilts on its axis away from the sun, around us falling more evidence of the sun's whispered secret—*I am leaving*—than we can hope to comprehend.

Yet we take another step, and another, because inside this sharp-tongued light, this harsher hue, is a new and ghostly kind of beauty: the beauty of autumn itself and the joy it portends, from smiling Jack-o-lanterns that will soon turn up on front steps everywhere, to the crisp cool air of afternoon walks by the river, to the bounty of Thanksgiving and families drawn near. The holidays are only a breath away.

All this, brought us this one single morning, with the bewitching way light falls differently.

And here we are, delivered to autumn.

Paul Baucom

Shadows and mist, Spanish moss and cypress thickets, the landscape surrounding Savannah inspires an eerie lyricism.

Amanda Brandt

Savannah's skyline reaches just above the trees. The height of new construction in the historic district is one of many architectural details carefully monitored by the Historic Review Board.

Bailey Davidson

Jonathan Slavkin

Bright lights, like this festive crown, indicate there is a party going on inside this City Market club. Musical choices on any night range from rock to jazz to blues.

Richard Rodriguez

Hair and makeup are all done. As a setting for blockbuster films, such as Forrest Gump *and* The Legend of Bagger Vance, *and with the growing reputation of late October's Savannah Film and Video Festival, the city has emerged as a center for moviemaking and celebration.*

Jonathan Slavkin

Urbane elegance can be found throughout the city. Extraordinary fountains —spouting swans, Tritons, and griffins—provide refreshing sounds.

Paul Baucom

Constructed early in the nineteenth century, Fort Pulaski served as a protection for Savannah during the early days of the Republic. Now the sounds of children and year-round visitors replace the roar of cannon fire.

Richard Rodriguez

Through the windows of the Trade Center, conventioneers have a beautiful view across the river past tugboats to the historic riverfront and the domes and the towers that create the skyline of downtown. On the right, one of the city's many art exhibits affords another view.

Isi Sarfati

Monuments in Forsyth Park and Colonial Cemetery—saluting patriots and heroes of America's past—look their best in autumn light.

Jason S. Klein

Paul Baucomb

Seth Adair

Wishful dreamers? Hooky players? The wonder of a riverboat docked on River Street enthralls children of all ages.

Just as she turns green on St. Patrick's Day, Savannah turns red, white and blue for our veterans in November.

Isi Sarfati

Thank
you !

Winter solstice. Surrounding marshes generate magical reflections of the skies above. Only in the Low Country can one be treated to a view such as this.

Christopher Rorrer

Winter

by **Margaret W. DeBolt**

SAVANNAH IS BEAUTIFUL IN ALL SEASONS OF THE YEAR, from the riotous colors of spring and the lush gardens of summer to the changing hues and increased tempo of living in autumn.

But winter is my favorite time, quieter and cooler, with the special joys of the holiday season. It is Christmas and Hanukkah and Kwanza, with gleaming candles and holly berries, the shops aglow in City Market and on River Street. It is the Downtown Neighborhood Association Holiday Tour of Homes, with bright wreaths on open doors, shared warmth and hospitality.

There is time to walk by the 1851 Unitarian Universalist Church on Troup Square and remember Boston-born James Lord Pierpont, son of an Abolitionist, who copyrighted the beloved winter song "Jingle Bells" while he was an organist here in 1857.

Another former Savannahian, Charles Wesley, gave us "Hark, the Herald Angels Sing," which he first titled "Hark, How All the Welkin Rings." As strolling groups of carolers pass under lighted windows, you may hear both tunes.

With winter comes observances unique to Savannah. There are drum rolls and blazing fires at Old Fort Jackson, as uniformed reenactors recall the last days of the Confederate fort with the approach of General Sherman in 1864.

Now, the bedroom at the Green-Meldrim House, where the general once slept, is a dressing room for brides who marry at St. John's Episcopal Church next door. Fort Pulaski, too, hosts a holiday eggnog party, recalling a time when it guarded the city against capture from the sea.

Walk the quiet trails at Wormsloe Historic Site and mingle with those in Colonial garb who are celebrating an eighteenth-century Christmas with music and cider and warm molasses cookies.

At Bethesda, another generation of youths brings in the Yule Log and cheerfully decorates the halls with greenery in the manner of those first Bethesda Boys of some 250 years ago.

New Year's Eve brings First Night at City Market, a family celebration with entertainment for all ages. At midnight, hundreds of balloons are released to drift into the courtyard on the revelry.

Late in January comes the Martin Luther King, Jr., parade, as the community remembers a great man who often visited here.

The Georgia Heritage Celebration in February sees a different kind of parade, as schoolchildren become Yamacraws or Colonials for a day and march down Bull Street to meet the mayor. All over the city, events honor Georgia founder James Edward Oglethorpe and those first brave settlers of 1733.

One can drive through the Savannah National Wildlife Refuge, where alligators bask in the sun and migrating birds refresh themselves. Walk the quiet beaches of Tybee, echoing now only to the cries of birds and waves breaking on the sand. Visit the winding nature trails at Skidaway Island State Park; admire the camellias blooming at Bonaventure and the hardy Alpine pansies in curbside gardens.

Winter is also a resting time, a peaceful interlude when one recalls the past and plans for the future as the earth lies dormant before another season of growth and change.

Richard Rodriguez

During the holiday season, the city echoes with the sounds of rejoicing.

Richard Rodriguez

The plantation life of Savannah's early settlers is re-enacted during the Colonial Christmas celebration at the Wormsloe Historic Site.

Richard Rodriguez

In the nineteenth century, Savannah's cemeteries were not only a place of mourning but also a destination for outings—even wintertime strolls. Laurel Grove and Bonaventure, two of the loveliest Victorian cemeteries in America, reveal a wide array of poignant tombstones and magnificent statuary, where December light casts long shadows.

Richard Rodriguez

Hugh Swingle

A rainy day might inspire a quick duck into one of the many churches on the city's squares. Savannah is a magical town that surprises and delights with its natural and man-made beauty.

Jonathan Slavkin

The austerity and artistry of the vaulting at Fort Pulaski are sublime.

Tom Powell

Martin Luther King, Jr., is honored in January with the city's first big parade of the year. Marching bands, floats, and individuals from throughout the community join in celebration.

Many Savannahians say their favorite season to visit Tybee Island is winter, when the only crowds at the beach are feathered.

Rene Cabrel

Like the tides, so, too, the seasons come, go and return again.

Amanda Brandt

Networks, Transportation & Communications

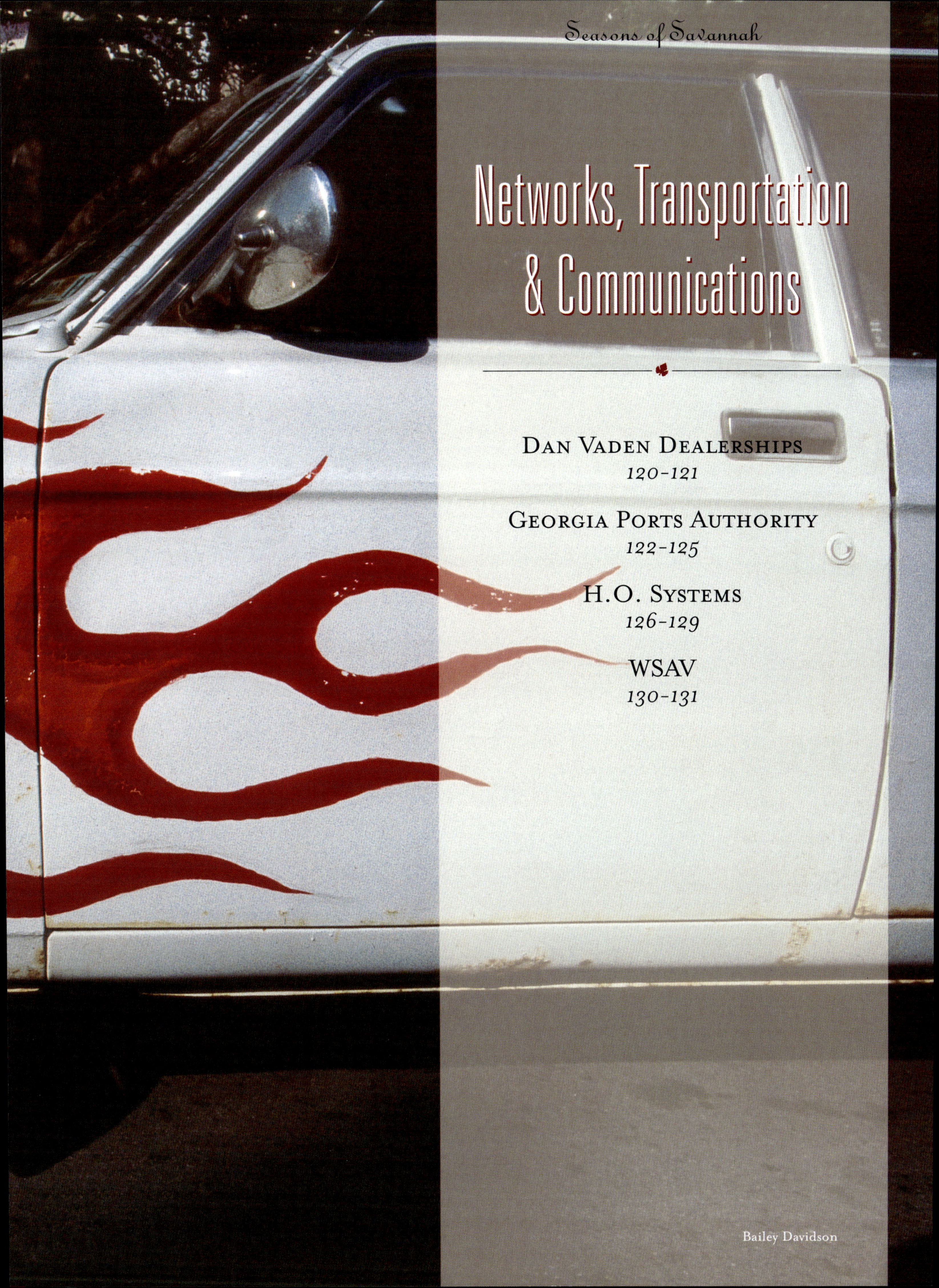

Bailey Davidson

Dan Vaden Dealerships

> *"Every day is a learning experience because no two cars and no two customers are alike."*

■ Dan Vaden Chevrolet was founded in 1968 and has grown to be one of the largest dealerships in the Southeast.

At age 73, Dan Vaden is a long way from retirement. While many of his contemporaries are thinking about slowing down, Vaden knows only one speed and that's fast. His great love for the automobile business is evident in each of the dealerships he owns and operates.

The Vaden Automotive Group includes Dan Vaden Chevrolet-Oldsmobile, Dan Vaden Chevy Truckland, Vaden Nissan, Vaden Volkswagen, Vaden Hyundai, Vaden Isuzu, Vaden Suzuki, and Dan Vaden Commercial Trucks in Savannah. Also part of the Dan Vaden family are Dan Vaden Chevy-Olds-Isuzu in Brunswick, Georgia, and Dan Vaden Hinesville.

Dan Vaden has 50 years of experience in the automobile business, but he says that, "every day is a learning experience because no two cars and no two customers are alike." He began his career as a used car sales trainee at Riverside Chevrolet in Jacksonville (now Nimnicht Chevrolet). His passion for selling vehicles made him a success at Riverside and he worked his way up over 17 years to become a partner in the business. There, he learned many of the skills needed to run his own business.

General Motors gave him the opportunity to put those skills to the test when they offered him the chance to become a Chevrolet dealer in Savannah in 1968. At that time, the area of Abercorn, which became home to Dan Vaden Chevrolet as well as many other businesses, was a dairy farm. It's difficult to imagine looking at Savannah's bustling Southside, but the first cars sold at Dan Vaden Chevrolet were sold on a dirt lot with the paperwork completed on the hood of the car.

■ The Dan Vaden family of dealerships owned and operated by (left to right) Peter Thacher, director of fixed operations; Dan Vaden, president; Bill Daniel, vice president; Jane Vaden Thacher, general manager.

■ Serving customers in the Coastal Empire for over 30 years.

As the city grew, so did Dan Vaden's business from one dealership to multiple franchises and locations. Vaden attributes much of his success to his employees, "Our business is a people business and our employees are an essential part of the equation. We treat our employees and our customers as partners in our business. Ultimately, they're responsible for our success."

Dan Vaden Chevrolet started with one employee—Dan Vaden himself. Today, the Vaden group employs about 350 people, including several family members. Vaden's daughter, Jane Vaden Thacher is the General Manager of Dan Vaden Chevrolet-Oldsmobile. His son-in-law, Bill Daniel, is the Vice President of the Vaden Group and his son-in-law, Peter Thacher, is director of fixed operations for the Vaden Group. While not officially an employee, his wife of 49 years, Jane Vaden, continues to be an integral part of Vaden's success. "I couldn't have done anything without her," he said.

Today, Vaden is focused on opportunities to grow the business. In 1999,he added the Oldsmobile franchise in Savannah and began construction on two new facilities. And at 73, Vaden is optimistic about his future in automobiles. "I'm really just getting started," he said.

■ Oldsmobile is the most recent addition to the Vaden dealership group joining Chevrolet, Nissan, Volkswagen, Isuzu, Hyundai, and Suzuki.

Georgia Ports Authority

The core business activity of the Georgia Ports Authority is facilitating international commerce.

■ As one of the premier ports in the world, the Port of Savannah consistently ranks as one of the top ten container ports in the United States. Photo by Jonas Jordan.

Savannah's picturesque river, cradled by flourishing wildlife and vegetation, is much more than just a popular tourist attraction. As magnificent ships pass the historic waterfront, thrilling curious visitors and local citizens alike, thousands of people upstream are hard at work at one of the top ten container ports in the United States. Facilities owned and operated by the Georgia Ports Authority in Savannah and Brunswick serve as efficient conduits for commerce and represent two of the most dynamic transportation systems in the world—linking water, rail, and highway infrastructure to benefit businesses and residents throughout the state.

This bustling operation on Savannah's shoreline began as a story authored by some of the state's most influential leaders. The Georgia General Assembly spearheaded the creation of the Georgia Ports Authority in 1945 with the express purpose of capitalizing on Georgia's natural attributes. Promoting the state's agricultural, industrial, and natural resources through the development, maintenance, and operation of deepwater and inland river port facilities, while maintaining the natural quality of the environment, remains the top priority of the Authority today.

For more than five decades, Georgia's ports have flourished and today, Georgia's deepwater ports in Savannah and Brunswick are world renowned for handling a vast array of cargo to destinations worldwide. In addition, the Port of Savannah plays an important role in support of our nation's defense and military preparedness.

Utilizing the state's natural resources further west, inland barge terminals in Bainbridge and Columbus are also operated under the auspices of the Georgia Ports Authority.

The core business activity of the Georgia Ports Authority is facilitating international commerce to and from locations around the world. Beyond that, port facilities statewide are valuable in terms of their economic productivity and vital in terms of the state's ability to compete successfully for international trade and investment opportunities.

■ The Port of Savannah offers service to more than 150 countries by more than 50 major steamship lines. Photo by Russ Bryant.

In an effort to stimulate statewide economic growth and opportunity and to further increase cargo volume via Georgia's ports, the Authority works full-time with organizations such as the Georgia Department of Industry, Trade and Tourism, economic development authorities, chambers of commerce, and governmental representatives to build an economic alliance of business partners throughout the state. Members of state and local business communities and representatives of maritime service organizations form a powerful alliance to assist in luring prospective customers and organizations to the state.

As a multi-million dollar enterprise, the Georgia Ports Authority serves as one of the state's most efficient and energetic economic facilitators. More than 80,000 jobs in Georgia are connected directly or indirectly to public and private port sector activities. Port related activities supporting these jobs are responsible for $1.8 billion in personal incomes, produce billions of dollars in sales revenue to benefit the state's bustling economy, and generate hundreds of millions of dollars in state and local tax receipts each year.

To remain competitive and productive, the Authority manages an ongoing program of environmentally responsible development programs based on sound research, realistic objectives and a firm understanding of market demand and future potential. This strategy has built Savannah into one of the most successful and efficient container ports in the United States. It has built the Port of Brunswick into one of the fastest growing and most respected auto handling ports on the eastern seaboard. This strategy has also propelled Georgia's ports into a position of dominance in the U.S. South Atlantic range for the handling of such general cargo as Georgia kaolin, Georgia forest products, and Georgia granite.

More than 60 steamship lines provide round-the-world services via Georgia's port facilities to Africa; Australia and New Zealand; the Caribbean and Islands of the Atlantic; Central America; the Far East, Indonesia and Malaysia; the Mediterranean; North Europe, the United Kingdom, Ireland, Scandinavia and Baltic; the Red Sea, Persian Gulf, India, Pakistan and Burma; and South America.

Georgia's dynamic and progressive ports will continue to serve as magnets for international trade while generating positive economic benefits for the citizens of Georgia for generations to come. The Georgia Ports Authority is committed to providing the state's importers and exporters with the most productive facilities and services on the U.S. East Coast. As Georgia's gateway to the world, the ports will continue to improve upon landside and harbor infrastructure, rail and road connections, advanced technology, and terminal services in order to encourage and advance the state's trade and investment opportunities.

The Port of Savannah's bustling harbor serves as a gateway to international trade. Photo by Diane L. Strickland.

Port of Savannah

In 1733, General James Oglethorpe set sail from England aboard the 220-ton *Anne* and landed on the shores he called Savannah. Upon the first settlers' arrival, they established a bulkhead against the northward expansion of the Spanish. The settlers' first export shipment to England consisted of 23 skins, three bottles of bear's oyl, and several parcels of sea root, snake root, rattlesnake root, sassafras, cenna root, shumack, and contravetta.

The trustees who governed the city offered a silver boat and spoon to the first child born in Georgia—the spoon a practical gift; the ship symbolic of the importance of the commercial link between the new colony and the Mother Country of England.

The first evidence of that relationship involved the cultivation of mulberry trees. Silkworms were imported to produce the silk needed to satisfy England's demand. While it never paid off, the experience helped Savannah recognize the value of reliance, flexibility, and innovation—qualities that still endure in this historic and majestic city today.

Following Georgia's break from England at the end of the Revolutionary War, Eli Whitney invented the cotton gin on what is today land owned by the Georgia Ports Authority. That invention launched the Port of Savannah into a top exporter of cotton. By the early 1800's, Savannah had earned the reputation as "King Cotton Port of the World," and the numbers reflected her success. In 1794, Savannah, with a population of 2,500, exported less than $500,000 worth of goods. Twenty-five years later it was the sixteenth largest city in the young nation with exports worth more than $14 million.

As the *S.S. Savannah*, the first steamship to cross the Atlantic Ocean, sailed from its waters on May 22, 1819, Savannah's port had added to its diversified trade portfolio rich cargoes of indigo, tobacco, and timber.

More than 80,000 jobs in Georgia are connected directly or indirectly to public and private port sector activities. Photo by Russ Bryant.

Georgia kaolin is one of many commodities exported via the Port of Savannah. Photo by Joseph Byrd.

Still, cotton reigned supreme. In 1855, exports from the Port of Savannah to all foreign destinations totaled more than $20 million, with cotton representing 89 percent of the total. Although Georgia's export activity waned during the five years of the Civil War, production increased shortly after the conflict ended in 1865. By the late 1870's, cotton production in the South had regained its pre-Civil War status and Savannah was the leading cotton exporter once more.

The first 10 years of the 20th Century brought continued rapid growth in trade for Georgia's exports. By 1905, Savannah's exports were greater than the combined exports of all other South Atlantic ports and by 1910, cotton comprised 90 percent of Brunswick's exports, and almost 85 percent of Savannah's. Similarly, Savannah was bringing in fertilizers, potash, nitrate of soda, sulfate of ammonia, aniline salts, and sulfur.

Since those early days of trade, Savannah has maintained and bolstered its leadership in maritime commerce—but not without some interruptions. The natural consequence of a worldwide depression sandwiched between two world wars occurred. More importantly, a domestic problem arose that could have a more far-reaching impact on the state's economy. A persistent and devastating insect—the boll weevil—wreaked havoc in Georgia's cotton fields, taking with it an export that still accounted for 80 percent of Georgia's total shipments.

Just as the world emerged from the depression in 1933, it began bracing for the second World War. This renewed activity fueled a resurgence for the Port of Savannah, once again proving its resilience and flexibility. The major difference was that cotton was no longer king with the commodity accounting for less than 15 percent of the total value of Savannah's exports. Just as had been the case 20 years earlier, the war and the corresponding boom following the war brought a flourishing business to the Port of Savannah in the 1940's.

Against that backdrop, the state created the Georgia Ports Authority in 1945 to oversee the development of Georgia's rich maritime resources in an innovative and progressive manner.

The state's vision became a reality when GPA seized the opportunity to buy the U.S. Army Quartermaster's Depot in Garden City, Georgia for $808,100 in 1948. The purchase of the 407-acre tract include 5.41 miles of warehouses and the wooden docks that had served as the embarkation point for the military during World War II. The wisdom of that investment has echoed through GPA's history, launching a new and modern era for the Port of Savannah.

Actual state port construction was not begun by the newly formed GPA until 1948 with the issuance of revenue bonds for $5.5 million. The Garden City facility, equipped with four general cargo berths, two 35-ton gantry cranes, three transit sheds and one tanker berth, officially opened for business in 1953. By the end of that year, the terminal had handled 232,920 tons of dry and liquid bulk cargo, servicing 46 vessels. Two years later, the Port of Savannah had outgrown the facility and expansion plans were underway.

To support the growing business, the Georgia Ports Authority acquired three miles of property downstream, on the western end of Savannah's city limits in 1958. The site, the former Ocean Steamship Terminal, was purchased for $2.8 million from the Central of Georgia Railway. The acquisition consisted of 87 acres of waterfront property served by the railroad. The Authority constructed three new berths, enlarged one of the slips and added a transit shed.

While those facilities were under construction, the Garden City Terminal was growing both in size and handling capability. In May 1959, the Georgia Ports Authority purchased the adjoining 388-acre Whitehall Plantation for $970,000. By this time, the Port of Savannah was serviced by five railways, five highways, and three airlines to boost its natural geographic access into the hinterland.

To keep up with the growing demand, three new berths were put into operation in 1962 at the

For more than five decades, Georgia's ports have flourished and today, Georgia's deepwater ports are renowned for handling a vast array of cargo to destinations worldwide. Photo by Russ Bryant.

Georgia Ports Authority's Garden City Terminal. That same year, Savannah saw a significant increase in export shipments. Along with pet food, poultry, and woodpulp, carpet had become one of the many commodities exported to destinations worldwide.

In 1965, the Georgia Ports Authority completed a 520,000 cubic foot cold storage warehouse at Garden City at the cost of $650,000. This was a tremendous advantage for Georgia peanut farmers and the seafood industry because Savannah now offered direct dockside storage for temperature-controlled cargoes.

Improvements continued at a rapid pace. In 1967, the United Nations issued a report that said, in part: "The rapidly expanding volume and velocity of trade has challenged the capacity of man to handle his business with greater economy and dispatch...Seaborne trade has grown steadily year after year...The ingenuity of man has met and is resolving the problems associated with this enormous traffic in goods...The movement of goods in international trade in containers, an innovation of the past two decades, is expanding rapidly..."

■ The Georgia Ports Authority is committed to the citizens of Georgia and Georgia businesses to develop strategies, nurture partnerships, and prepare port facilities that will propel the Port of Savannah into one of the most dynamic, efficient, and respected ports in the world. Photo by Jonas Jordan.

The U.N. report captured a concept soon to revolutionize logistics and transform the Port of Savannah into a bustling containerport. International trade was evolving into a seamless, integrated movement taking full advantage of the individual strengths and capabilities of ship, rail, and highway services.

The Georgia Ports Authority anticipated market changes and initiated yet another series of enhancements for the Port of Savannah with the addition of one container berth, 20 acres of paved container storage and the Authority's first container crane. On May 13, 1972, Seatrain Lines' *Visurgis* became the first full containership to call the Port of Savannah's Garden City Terminal.

From these origins, the Port of Savannah has emerged as one of the premier ports in the world, offering service to more than 150 countries by more than 50 major steamship lines and consistently ranking as one of the top 10 container ports in the United States. The two terminal facilities in Savannah feature nearly 1,300 acres of terminal area, close to three miles of berthing space for vessels, over three million square feet of covered storage and an ample supply of cranes and cargo handling equipment.

Today, international shippers and organizations from around the globe utilize Savannah's world-class facilities. Major imports handled via Savannah's port facilities include iron, steel, machinery, plywood, cocoa beans, granite, lumber, foodstuffs, anhydrous ammonia, chemicals, vegetable oil, asphalt, pig iron, and petroleum products. Top exports include kaolin clay, linerboard, machinery, woodpulp, military supplies and equipment, lumber and foodstuffs, tall oil, and petroleum products.

■ Port related activities in Georgia are responsible for $1.8 billion in personal incomes, produce billions of dollars in sales revenue to benefit the state's economy and generate hundreds of millions of dollars in state and local tax receipts each year. Photo by Diane L. Strickland.

For more than a decade, the Port of Savannah has demonstrated consistent and progressive growth in the volume of cargo handled via Savannah's Garden City Terminal and Ocean Terminal.

The Georgia Ports Authority is proud of its many accomplishments. However, the Authority must continue to implement new services, technologies, and facilities to increase its competitive edge in vying for cargo opportunities in the United States.

To remain competitive, the Georgia Ports Authority will continue to focus on the diversity of the marketplace and serve the dynamic needs of international customers. The Authority is committed to keeping alive its commitments to the citizens of Georgia and Georgia businesses to develop strategies, nurture partnerships, and prepare port facilities that will propel the Port of Savannah into one of the most dynamic, efficient, and respected ports in the world.

H.O. Systems

H.O. Systems produces and supports mission-critical billing software to the telecommunications industry.

Savannah's historic district—framed by live oaks drenched with Spanish moss—is filled with secrets. There are monuments honoring Civil War heroes, homes boasting architectural elegance, and restaurants serving nationally acclaimed cuisine. Amid this serene picture of life in the Old South lies a fast-paced company that is becoming one of the nation's leading providers of billing and customer care business systems for wireless carriers.

From its headquarters in a stately commerce building renamed eCommerce Building, H.O. Systems produces and supports mission-critical billing software to the telecommunications industry. With a mission statement declaring "Service Beyond Software," as its driving force, the company's position in the market has continued to climb through the years as evidenced by its fascinating history. Over the past decade, sales growth has skyrocketed with projections for the future even more optimistic. With a client coverage in most of the United States, H.O. Systems' impressive list of clientele has spread the word

H.O. Systems President, S. Hart Williford.

Jennifer Mathis, V.P. Corporate Development discussing long-term communications strategies.

of the Savannah company's innovative products and services and kept the company ahead of its competition.

Founded more than a decade ago in response to the needs of the thriving cellular communications industry, this Savannah based company has gone from one customer in its first location—a private home—to more than 200 full-time employees and a modern facility discreetly located in historic downtown Savannah. The growth of this high-tech company is so phenomenal, that it has attracted the attention of local leaders such as Business, Education and Technology Alliance (BETA), Savannah Chamber of Commerce, and Savannah Morning News. Recently, H.O. Systems was the recipient of the top manufacturing award within an 11-county area based on revenue growth, growth in resources and commitment to the community by the Georgia Economic Development Association.

S. Hart Williford, H.O. Systems president, said the sound reputation earned at H.O. Systems is the result of satisfied customers referring others in the industry. With Savannah as its headquarters, Williford said, employees are easy to attract and keep.

He adds, "Savannah is our company's home. It is a great location for us and people love to move here. We have great partnerships with schools, including Georgia Tech, Armstrong Atlantic State University, Savannah State University, and Georgia Southern University. We also utilize services and students from the Savannah College of Art and Design. We use

Members of H.O. Systems Emerging Technologies department.

H.O. Systems Leadership Team: Jennifer Mathis, Vice President, Corporate Development; Glenn Gibney, Vice President, Sales and Account Management; Tammy Cannon, Vice President, Client Services; S. Hart Williford, President, H. O. Systems; Maria Watts, Vice President, Strategic Planning; Jerry Record, Vice President Product Support and Integration; and Dave Peterson, Vice President, Application Support.

Customer, Hargray Wireless, headquartered in Hilton Head, South Carolina.

a significant number of interns onsite and use faculty at the specific institutions to teach classes and assist us in night school and we are near enough to Jacksonville, Washington, and Atlanta to significantly recruit from those cities. The quality of living here is fantastic! Our turnover rate is a low 3 percent!" he added.

That growth has led to the addition of several new customers, including Dobson Cellular Systems of Oklahoma City, Leap Wireless International of San Diego, First Cellular of Southern Illinois, Price Communications of Atlanta, and Suncom of Jackson, Mississippi.

"I attribute our growth to the fact that our company is a very aggressive company that wants to grow and maintain our position as dominant player in the industry. There are a lot of companies that promote good products, but what we excel in is our service. Additionally, the journey we're on will give a higher return on investment. Most customers use only a fraction of the functionality of the software they select. We pride ourselves in partnering with our customers to ensure the highest utilization of the software features to achieve their business strategies. We offer a high level of training and we get to know our customers," he said.

H.O. Systems' online training for new customers.

H.O. Systems e-Commerce building.

Quality products and equipment is another important aspect of H.O. Systems' successful philosophy. "We have a huge commitment to quality. Anything we send out to a customer has gone through rigorous quality control testing," Williford said.

Founded in 1988, it is the company's cutting edge technology that has led to exciting new breakthroughs in the fast paced everchanging telecommunications industry. For instance, in 1999, a new generation of web-based next generation suite of products that brings e-business solutions to all client partners was introduced, paving the way for Electronic Bill Presentment and Payment. In July of 2000, the company unveiled Speedsuite, a web-based billing system that allows customers to access their billing system via the web.

Partnering with more than 3 million subscribers per month, the company's growth led to the purchase of a 50,000 square foot facility in downtown Savannah that has been called "eCommerce Building" to reflect the company's commitment to advanced technological development. And to strengthen its commitment to the community, H.O. Systems' employees contribute to more than 20 local charitable organizations, including Habitat for Humanity, The Red Cross, and the Ronald McDonald House. Additionally, the company is a member of the Trustees Council of the Savannah Area Chamber of Commerce and BETA, the Business, Education, and Technology Alliance whose goal is to attract more high-tech businesses to the Savannah area.

With the support of major industry associations such as The Cellular Technology Industry Association and Personal Communications Industry Association, H.O. Systems maintains an annual membership in both and has made appearances at a variety of trade shows where its presence has brought both new customers and increased awareness of its products and services. In fact, in 1999, the company unveiled a two-story, 1500 square foot demonstration and display booth to communicate its mission at CTIA.

With strategic partnerships with selected industry leaders such as Output Technology Solutions, Compaq, Macromedia, Empower for Wireless, Cellstar, Rateintegration, Oracle, IBM, and H.O.'s sister company, GiantBear.com, H.O. Systems is able to combine technology with influence to generate even more of a national presence.

With a bright future ahead, Williford attributed the past success of the company to its dedicated group of employees. "Above all else, we have great people working here. We commit to hiring the best employees—the ones who are going to see us through the years. The last five years, we've doubled in size. Our company has moved up to handle much larger companies. We look forward to what lies ahead."

WSAV

Experienced anchors and reporters have become television favorites to viewers.

The NBC affiliate that once brought the humor of Bob Hope and the romance of Johnny Mercer into the living rooms of Savannah's radio listeners in 1939, is also the station that introduced the area's residents to the world through television. Although years have passed, some things haven't changed. The energetic television station that first drew listeners to a quality level of sound is still bringing first-class entertainment and high-quality news to Savannahians through a new generation of technology. Thousands who tune in daily couldn't be more pleased with the station's progress.

■ Stan Crumley, President and General Manager of WSAV-TV.

It's not just the upscale news set, fast-paced music, and warm, professional newscasters that makes WSAV-TV's news a favorite of Coastal Empire and Low Country viewers. Since 1997, WSAV's strengths can be attributed to its ownership by Media General, Inc. An independent, publicly-owned communications company, Media General is responsible for the operation of 25 other network-affiliated television stations, 100 weekly newspapers, and 21 daily newspapers. WSAV now has the backing of a mega-giant in the communications world. Media General's size and scope have allowed Savannah's television audience to welcome the highest technology and most current events into their home as spontaneously as the news happens.

Stan Crumley, President and General Manager of WSAV, credited Media General for allowing the Savannah station to broadcast quality news and entertainment. "The breadth of Media General's holdings is crucial in today's broadcasting environment and provides WSAV with the most modern broadcasting technology available in the industry, and in the Savannah community," he said. "Media General recognizes that in order to remain a robust member of the communications industry, it must not only consider how technology affects the industry in general, and WSAV in particular, but also how technology is changing the way viewers and advertisers use its product."

■ WSAV is located at 1430 East Victory Drive in Savannah.

■ WSAV's news anchors Tina Tyus-Shaw and Michael Jordan are two television favorites in the Savannah area.

In its early days, as viewers followed the progress of the Allies in World War II through WSAV radio, a need for expanded coverage soon became evident. In 1947, WSAV radio upgraded its power to 5,000 watts and expanded its coverage of important local news, weather, and sports to include the Coastal Empire of Georgia and the Low Country of South Carolina. As the definition of "local" grew, so did WSAV's broadcast capabilities.

Nine years later, in 1956, WSAV used the same popular call letters to bring television into the homes of its listeners. Those first telecasts aired from the original radio studios atop The Liberty National Bank building on Broughton Street, and the flashing WSAV sign became a well-known downtown landmark for many years. The station soon relocated to palm-tree lined "World Famous Victory Drive" in 1960, where a new broadcast tower and professional studio facility had been built. The new tower spread WSAV into surrounding counties in Georgia and South Carolina and introduced thousands of viewers to The NBC Television Network. The station continues to broadcast from that location today and residents have learned to recognize its familiar facade as they travel to and from work.

The same philosophy of success that spawned its popularity in those early years is still evident in WSAV's programming today. Viewers who once enjoy local and worldwide news, weather, and sports are now treated to even more of the same with three full hours of daily updates. Experienced anchors, reporters, and news photographers have become familiar to viewers, and coverage has expanded to include contemporary issues in the lives of Savannahians.

Striving for excellence has paid off, according to Crumley. In 1999, the Georgia Associated Press named WSAV-TV/News 3 the Pacemaker Award winner for best local news coverage. WSAV also earned AP awards for best sports coverage, best sports program, best sports reporting, and the best use of sound.

"As the recipient of awards that recognize WSAV's outstanding news operation, our pride is evident," Crumley said. "But the challenge to continue our daily drive for excellence is still growing."

■ The WSAV Microwave Van allows the Savannah citizens to benefit from quick, up-to-date news in the area.

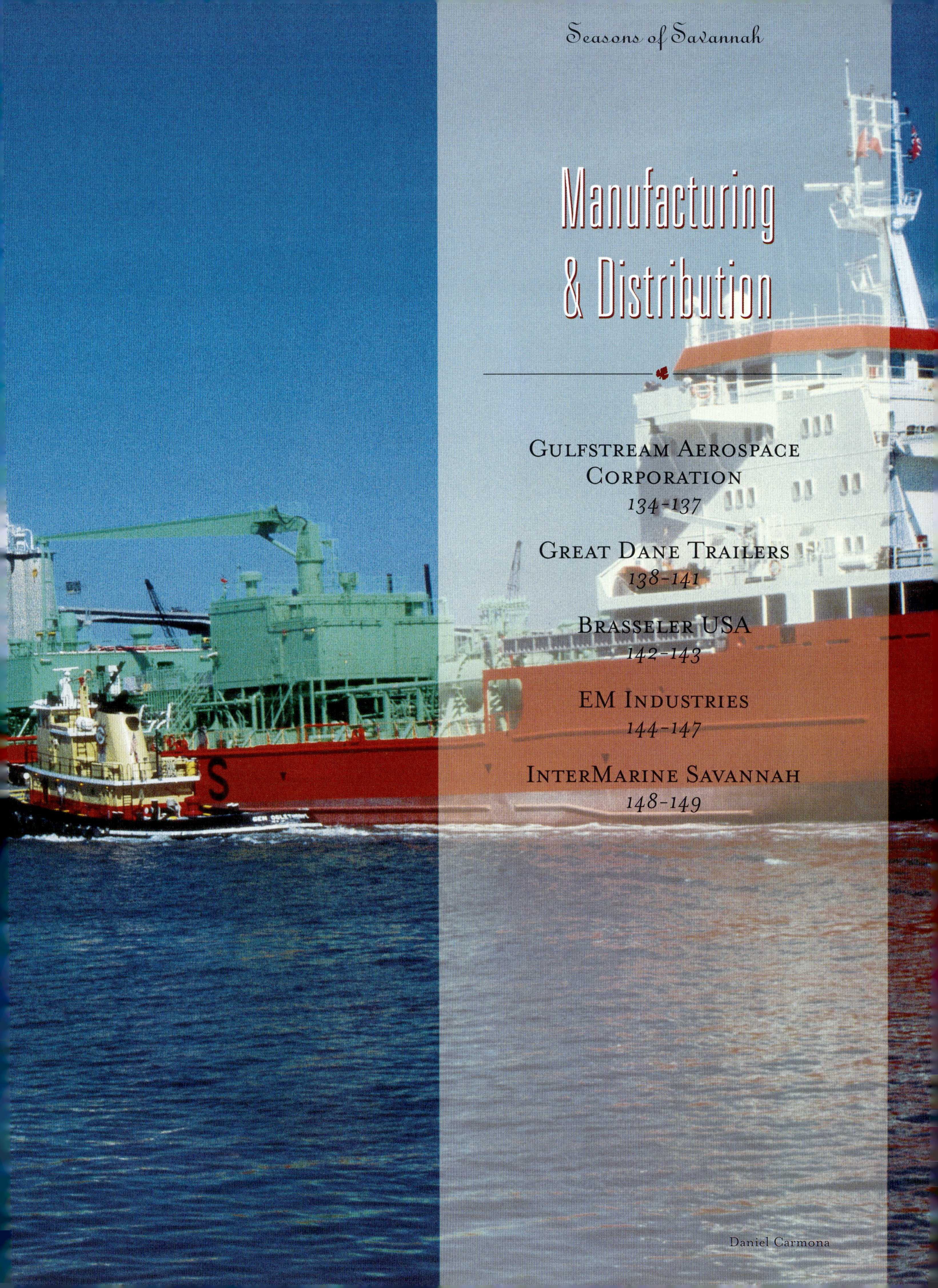

Manufacturing & Distribution

Daniel Carmona

Gulfstream Aerospace Corporation

Gulfstream has produced more than 1,100 aircraft for corporate, government, private, and military customers worldwide.

From the air, the company's vast facilities framed with sleek aircraft aligned to perfection spark the curiosity of newcomers. When those visitors step off a commercial jet landing at the Savannah International Airport their curiosity is satisfied. As they head toward the terminal from their arriving gate, they are greeted with a sense of pride the city has for its largest employer (boasting more than 8,300 employees). A brightly colored banner emblazoned with the company's most amazing achievement—the Gulfstream V—spans the width of the long hallway and proudly proclaims Savannah as the home of Gulfstream Aerospace Corporation.

Much like its home city—historic Savannah—Gulfstream's milestones have filled the history books, and publications worldwide have illustrated the company's dominance in the global market of business jets.

Technological superiority has led to an impressive list of accomplishments that reads like an encyclopedia of amazing discoveries. Since its beginnings in 1958, Gulfstream has produced more than 1,100 aircraft for corporate, government, private, and military customers worldwide and its prestigious list of satisfied clientele is constantly expanding.

Luxurious and efficient—Gulfstream cabins are an office in the sky.

Chatham County's largest industrial employer broke production records in 1999 and it was that year that the company rolled out its 100th Gulfstream V jet to a runway lined with eager onlookers. Just a few weeks prior to that historic occasion, the company announced the opening of a new 53,650-square-foot refurbishment and completions support facility while across the country, a satisfied corporate jet customer appeared on national television touting the company's first sale of a GV aircraft over the internet. During the summer of 2000, the company was awarded a firm-fixed-price contract to supply two Gulfstream IV-SPs to the Arab Republic of Egypt Air Force. The aircraft will provide worldwide airlift for Egyptian government officials.

The ultra-long range Gulfstream V.

"Gulfstream currently has 74 aircraft in the Middle East and North Africa and over the next two years we expect our fleet in these areas to grow substantially," said Ernest Edwards, Gulfstream vice president, international sales.

Other international customers include Kuwait, which received the first of three Gulfstream V's in November 1999 and Saudi Arabia, which ordered a Gulfstream IV-SP and its first special mission version of the Gulfstream V in 1998 specifically for medical evacuation. Also in 1998, Gulfstream signed a $335 million contract for 12 Gulfstream IV-SP aircraft with National Air Service (NAS) to establish the Middle East Shares program. With such worldwide notoriety, one might be surprised to learn that that the company's claim to fame was heightened with the creation of the Gulfstream IV and then the Gulfstream V, the world's first ultra-long range, large-cabin business jet. In 1998,

Gulfstream and the GV Industry Team were awarded the prestigious 1997 Robert J. Collier Trophy by the National Aeronautic Association, widely recognized as the top honor in aviation. (Past recipients include Orville Wright, Charles "Chuck" Yeager, Neil A. Armstrong, and the Apollo 11 flight crew, Cessna and Boeing.)

By mid-2000, the Gulfstream IV/Gulfstream IV-SP fleet had accumulated more than 1.2 million hours of flight time and holds 74 world and national flight records. While the GV continues to set records, the legendary GIV continues to be the world's best-selling large-cabin, long-range business jet. Since it was introduced in 1985, Gulfstream has focused on continuous technology improvements that are substantiated by its customers. More than 80 Fortune 500 companies use the GIV to meet extensive and diverse corporate travel needs and according to Bryan Moss, Gulfstream chairman, the GIV's record speaks for itself:

"The GIV's proven advanced technology continues to provide exceptional customer value with its reliability, increased safety, and decreasing operating costs. The Gulfstream IV's success is reflected by its continued strong sales and its record of reliable service around the world," he said.

■ Gulfstream customers can choose from a wide variety of leathers, fabrics, and carpets to complement the custom interiors of their aircraft.

The Gulfstream IV's successor, the Gulfstream V, boasts records of its own. Capable of flying 6,500 nautical miles at speeds up to Mach .885 and cruise at altitudes up to 51,000 feet, this popular jet quickly swept the world with its efficient reputation. Powered by two Rolls-Royce BR710 turbofan engines, the Gulfstream V is the only ultra-long range aircraft that allows passengers to enjoy a maximum cabin altitude of only 6,000 feet and a 100 percent fresh air ventilation system. As of the summer of 2000, the Gulfstream V had set a total of 65 official world and national records for distance and speed.

The success of Gulfstream's current aircraft line has never been stronger. With more than 90 Gulfstream V's in customer service and a 110 aircraft, $3.5 billion backlog for the GV and GIV-SP (in the year 2000 alone), Gulfstream aircraft continue to be the world's best-selling large-cabin, long- and ultra-long-range business aircraft.

"The market has made a clear choice in favor of the Gulfstream V in the ultra-long-range, large-cabin class of business aircraft," said Bill Boisture, the company's president and chief operating officer. "The Gulfstream V has met and often exceeded every goal we had for the program when it was launched."

To meet the aviation needs of its customers, Gulfstream also offers a full range of aircraft products and services, including the Gulfstream IV-SP®, the ultra-long range Gulfstream V®, Gulfstream Shares®, Gulfstream Financial Services, Gulfstream Lease℠, Gulfstream Pre-Owned Aircraft Sales™, Gulfstream Charter Services®, Gulfstream Management Services℠, and Gulfstream ServiceCare®. The company employs more than 8,300 people at eight locations and a sophisticated website (www.gulfstream.com) offers photos of Gulfstream aircraft and related information. A wholly-owned subsidiary of General Dynamics (which is headquartered in Falls Church, Virginia) that corporation employs approximately 43,000

■ The Gulfstream IV-SP, the world's best-selling large cabin, long-range business jet.

people worldwide and has annualized sales of approximately $10 billion.

And while Savannah has celebrated the company's continued prosperity, across the globe, Gulfstream's dominance has soared. In Singapore, the celebrated delivery of a fifth Gulfstream IV-MPA (multi-purpose version of the Gulfstream IV-SP aircraft) to the Japanese Air Self Defense Force was met with eagerness. The aircraft, designated the U-4 in Japan, is equipped with a multi-mission, rapid-change interior for a variety of roles. Its advanced technology will become an international defense breakthrough. In short, Gulfstream Aerospace Corporation's decade of the '90s spilled out into the new millennium with a forceful presence.

■ Gulfstream service is one of the company's fastest growing business segments.

"Over the 42-year history of our company, Gulfstream aircraft have earned the reputation as the world standard for safety, reliability, technical superiority, comfort, and performance in the large-cabin, long-range market," said Boisture.

While the company remains an industry giant, it is also one of southeast Georgia's friendliest and most philanthropic employers. As an avid supporter of the arts—including major charitable organizations—Gulfstream has sponsored a variety of concerts, festivals, and special events in the area. And while it has provided aircraft and support for more than 35 nations and become the leading designer, developer, manufacturer, and marketer of the world's most popular business jet aircraft, it has continually strengthened its ties with the community. Other contributions include the donation of 5,500 square yards of carpet to local organizations such as the St. Martin Deporres Society (Kids Café), the Girl Scouts Council, Memorial Day School, and the Bethesda Youth Organization, among others.

■ The Gulfstream V is an efficient form of transportation whether flying across the U.S. or flying New York to Tokyo non-stop.

But the creativity of the Gulfstream team is not limited to just sales of its aircraft. More recently, the company announced plans for a unique form of personal service. By establishing a worldwide concierge service, one call will provide a customer with worldwide reservations for transportation, accommodations, sporting events, leisure, and recreational activities.

Another aspect of the Gulfstream's customer service level is the development of a customer value model that highlights critical factors that determine their priorities and preferences. The metrics derived from this model rank customer priorities and provide the company with a road map for improvement.

"The customer value model will become one of our most important tools to elevate Gulfstream's performance in the eyes of our customers," said Larry Flynn, Gulfstream's senior vice president of aircraft services.

To further enhance the flow of information to and from customers, Gulfstream has launched e.Gulfstream and is designing customized websites for each customer. Customers will receive unprecedented real-time information about their

■ The craftsmanship of Gulfstream interiors is world-renowned for its quality and finish.

aircraft including digital images during the build and completion process. With these electronic initiatives, Gulfstream's objectives are both customer and prospect focused.

"Gulfstream will improve the flow of information to people considering a Gulfstream and those who already own one," said Boisture. "It will expand our ability to build, manage, and maintain customer relationships and consolidate data specifically for each customer. e.Gulfstream defines our move toward becoming an e.Business."

With a past so rich with achievements, the future brings excitement for the Gulfstream industry.

"Gulfstream's legacy is a testimony to the excellence of its aircraft and the professionalism of the people who produce them. Over the 42-year history of the company, Gulfstream aircraft have earned the reputation as the world standard for safety, reliability, technical superiority, comfort, and performance. With a past so rich with achievements and a backlog of orders over $3 billion, Gulfstream's future is secure as one of the most widely known and respected brands in the world."

■ Gulfstream Aerospace will continue its leadership and set the standard for the future of business aviation.

Great Dane Trailers

In Savannah, the Great Dane name stands as one of the city's most significant strengths.

■ 1931, one of the first Great Dane van trailers hitched to a vintage Studebaker truck/tractor.

When you pass a sleek and gleaming trailer on the road, chances are, the trailer and its mud flaps will bear the logo of Great Dane Trailers, a name that is renowned throughout the nation and the world.

In Savannah, the Great Dane name stands as one of the city's most significant strengths.

With the massive cable-span bridge towering in its background, Savannah's Great Dane Trailers' facility is linked to the city's great historic district by a four-lane viaduct. It is the profile of that plant, sitting at the foot of America's first planned city, that links it to the community with advanced technology and a history of outstanding business values. Those same ideals that created the company one hundred years ago are still evident in the company's modern facilities, but time and technology have enhanced Great Dane's products, making them the leader among long-lasting, better-built trailers.

Today's trailers are the result of highly skilled engineers using space-age technology. Once a design is approved, a prototype is built and tested on the most advanced, computer-driven road simulator in the industry. This multi-million dollar test device can expose a trailer to an equivalent of ten years of real world wear and tear in less than ten days. It is this commitment to product testing that assures the customer of the highest return on their equipment investment.

During Great Dane Trailers' evolution from a steel fabricating company founded in 1900, two goals have driven the company—building superior products and fulfilling customer needs. And through the years, Great Dane management has never lost sight of those ideals. With the focus on quality, the goal has always been to be the best.

■ 2000, Great Dane freight van with logo symbolizing the company's 100th Anniversary.

■ Original headquarters of the Steel Products Company, circa 1920.

The story of Great Dane's success begins in the early 1900s when sheet metal blowpipe systems were prevalent at sawmills, planing mills, and furniture plants throughout the southeast. Many of these dust- and chip-collecting systems were fabricated at the Savannah Blowpipe Company and transported and erected throughout the region. Established in Savannah, with a total capitalization of $3,000 it was that company that set the standards for today's Great Dane.

By 1912, the Savannah Blowpipe Company had begun to fabricate light structural steel and steel plate products. In 1931, Savannah Blowpipe was incorporated as The Steel Products Company, boasting total assets of more than $100,000. Sensing an economic opportunity inherent in the development of better highways throughout the Southeast, the new corporation decided to design and manufacture truck trailers for over-the-road freight hauling. To implement this decision, The Steel Products Company hired the best trailer man in the industry. The best of the breed were being built by a Greenville, South Carolina, man, who, in 1930, began calling them by the name, "Great Dane." He had been familiar with the use of Great Dane dogs in Belgium and other European countries as work animals and admired them for their strength and stamina, two icons of today's Great Dane products. "And thus began the legend of these quality trailers."

A market for lighter-weight trailers gradually developed through economic pressures and the advent of highway weight laws aimed at haulers were implemented. In 1938, The Steel Products Company responded to this new opportunity with lightweight tank trailers and van trailers made of high tensile steel. A stressed-skin van of exceptionally lightweight design became the principal Great Dane product.

War-time was a profitable era for Great Dane. Steel Products produced nearly 12,000 trailers on government contracts during World War II and was awarded the Army-Navy "E" for excellence in quality and construction five separate times. The sales distribution gaps between the Southeast and Northeast were soon closed, and Great Dane distributorships began invading the Midwest. A turning point in the company came when research and development teams pioneered the refrigerated trailer field.

In the early '40s, they introduced the first produce van with a wet ice bunker and a gas engine and blower system, which was soon followed by the first factory-finished refrigerated van. The Great Dane reefer, as this type of trailer came to be known, has never relinquished its leadership.

By 1949, the Steel Products Company again responded to an economic opportunity, this time with a van trailer made of aluminum and with a tandem axle. And in 1953, refrigerated aluminum trailers were in demand for use in the Florida perishables market and became the standard for the eastern United States.

■ In the early 1940's Great Dane built the first produce van with a wet ice bunker and a gas engine and blower system, which was soon followed by the first factory finished refrigerated van.

■ GREAT DANE ENTERED THE PIGGYBACK AND CONTAINER MARKET IN 1961.

Sales outlets had been established in 31 cities and 18 states throughout the eastern half of the United States.

In 1958, The Steel Products Company changed its name to Great Dane Trailers, Inc. The following year, Great Dane brought out a redesigned line of van trailers and perfected a new tank trailer line, both largely of lightweight aluminum. As these new trailers again won widespread acceptance, it was decided to phase out all structural steel products and further expand trailer production. Great Dane was finally in the truck trailer business 100 percent!

Great Dane entered the piggyback and container market, completing its first piggyback trailer order in 1961 and its first maritime container order in 1963. Sales outlets had been established in 24 states blanketing the eastern half of the country.

In 1966, Great Dane announced a $2 million expansion program, which increased trailer production 100 percent. And in 1972, Great Dane acquired a second manufacturing facility by purchasing Arrow Trailers in Memphis, Tennessee.

Today, all platform trailers are constructed at this plant. Since this time, production at the Memphis plant has increased by almost 200 percent.

In 1974 following a period of unprecedented increases in production, a decision was made to build yet another manufacturing facility for van trailers. Brazil, Indiana was selected as the location for this plant, due to its centralized location to serve the western and midwestern trailer markets. Simultaneously, expansion and innovations in insulating methods at the Savannah plant further expanded its capacity for reefers.

The decision was made to almost double the Brazil facility by adding a refrigerated trailer production line, completed during the first quarter of 1978. Expansion and improvement soon became everyday words and quality a way of life. Great Dane experienced explosive growth in the 1980s that allowed great strides in trailer technology and more efficient service to customers.

During 1988, the company acquired the SuperSeal reefer product line and the Wayne, Nebraska Plant from Timpte, creating the broadest line of reefers in the industry. Great Dane installed computer controlled Road Simulation Equipment in the Research and Development Lab, located in the Savannah plant—the only one operational today. This was followed closely by the use of Finite Element Analysis software, key in achieving optimum strength-to-weight designs. The nineties brought even more advances. In 1996, Great Dane opened a dry van plant in Terre Haute, Indiana, as well as a parts distribution center adjacent to it. With 1997 came a merger of Great Dane and Pines Trailer, creating Great Dane Limited Partnership—the world's largest trailer company.

■ EARLY REFRIGERATED TRAILERS MADE LONG DISTANCE SHIPPING OF FRUITS AND VEGETABLES POSSIBLE.

State-of-the-art computer equipment and technology reinforce Great Dane's position as the industry leader in innovation and quality design.

Sales outlets consisting of dealerships and company-owned branches stretch from coast-to-coast across the U.S., into Canada, Mexico, and South America.

In June 2000, Great Dane announced plans to expand its manufacturing capabilities into Canada. The new plant will be located in Quinte West, Ontario. In its first phase, the plant will be some 300,000 square feet and will employ 500 people when operational.

This state-of-the-art facility will have the capacity to produce 6,000-plus trailers annually, and will serve markets across Canada and the northeast region of the United States.

A visit to one of Great Dane's manufacturing facilities often amazes even veteran trailer buyers. An old-fashioned work ethic is prevalent. Pride in workmanship abounds. Manufacturing tolerances are tight. Banners everywhere state, "Our Customers Pay for the Best. It Is Up To Us To See That They Get It."

Quality cannot be inspected into a product after completion. All workers are responsible for their own quality control and deficiencies must be corrected before the trailer advances further.

As a final step, each trailer travels down a final inspection line. On this line, every detail is checked again. All imperfections are corrected before a Quality Control decal is signed and affixed. The, and only then, is a trailer released to its owner.

That impressive facility is a typical phenomenon of the American economy—a small business that grew and changed as the country offered opportunity for profitable change. It has been the commitment to consistent quality and innovation that has indeed made Great Dane the industry leader. And it is these same principles that will drive Great Dane Trailers into the next century.

Division headquarters of Great Dane Trailers located on the corner of Bay Street and Lathrop Avenue.

Brasseler USA

From the selection of the finest raw materials to the use of the most exacting manufacturing technologies and microscopic inspections, Brasseler USA instruments have become standard tools in a variety of professions.

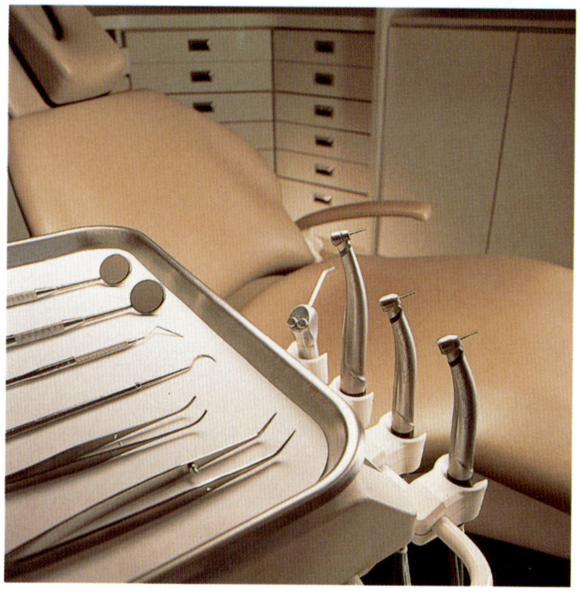

While tourists and residents thrive on Savannah's historic charm and aesthetic ambiance, the city also boasts an internationally known industry giant in the world of dental, medical, and industrial rotary cutting instruments. Brasseler USA is headquartered in a modern facility located on the city's expanding southside. When considered with its European affiliates, Brasseler is the largest rotary instrument manufacturer in the world serving more than 120 countries. Savannah has benefited from Brasseler USA's prosperity since 1980 and has continued to carry on the traditions started by the Brasseler family in 1923.

■ Brasseler USA has earned a reputation for designing and developing unique rotary cutting instruments for the dental professional.

The interesting history began in 1923 when Peter Brasseler I and his brothers established Gebrueder Brasseler (translated to "Brasseler Brothers" in English) for the production of dental rotary instruments distributed under the Komet brand in Düsseldorf, Germany. The Company headquarters was rebuilt in Lemgo in 1945, following the war. Peter Brasseler I could not sell his products via specialized dealers and decided to supply his customers directly. This unique distribution system for high quality innovative products would prove over time to be among Brasseler's greatest competitive advantages. The founder's son, Peter Brasseler II, joined the family business and worked diligently to establish markets throughout Europe and Asia before he personally founded Brasseler USA in 1976.

The United States' sales and marketing department was originally located in Chicago, Illinois. However, following the introduction of the first tungsten carbide bur worldwide, Mr. Brasseler chose to create a manufacturing plant and distribution center in Savannah, Georgia after entering the U.S. market. A strong skilled labor force, developed highways and port facilities, an international airport, along with ideal weather conditions allowing for year-round production made Savannah an appealing location.

■ Absolute accuracy is guaranteed from instrument to instrument, ensuring that the Brasseler USA name means quality.

Recently renovated facilities in Savannah employ more than 225 residents of Savannah and neighboring communities. As home to Brasseler USA's administrative offices, the Savannah complex includes sales, marketing, advertising, finance, customer service, data processing, manufacturing, and distribution facilities. Within the impressive 85,000-square-foot complex, millions of rotary instruments are manufactured and imported for distribution throughout the markets served by Brasseler USA.

As the company continues to provide its customers with the highest level of satisfaction, Brasseler USA excels by providing the most innovative product design and development in the industry. Noted for their precision and durability, along with the ability to operate efficiently with a highly sensitive touch, the company incorporates a multi-tiered approach to its product design. From the selection of the finest raw materials to the use of the most exacting manufacturing technologies and microscopic inspections, Brasseler USA instruments have become standard tools in a variety of professions. The company's customers range in subject areas from dental offices to hospital operating rooms to aerospace manufacturing. Instruments designed, manufactured, and distributed include rotary diamond, carbide abrasives, and polishing instruments, surgical saw blades and high-speed neuro drill systems. A growing number of customers encompass the fine arts, including stone, glass and metal engravers, jewelers, and cosmetic nail technicians.

One area of particular pride for the company's President and Chief Executive Officer, Don Waters, a Savannah native, is in the area of dental rotary instruments. "Our long-standing tradition of innovation and creative thinking continues to grow at Brasseler USA. We have earned a reputation for designing and developing unique rotary instruments for the dental professional." Brasseler USA places a high value on research and development that results in products that surpasses its customers' expectations. Working with internationally renowned clinicians and thought leaders and the unique direct relationship with its dentist clients enables Brasseler USA to offer a product line that places it years ahead of its competition.

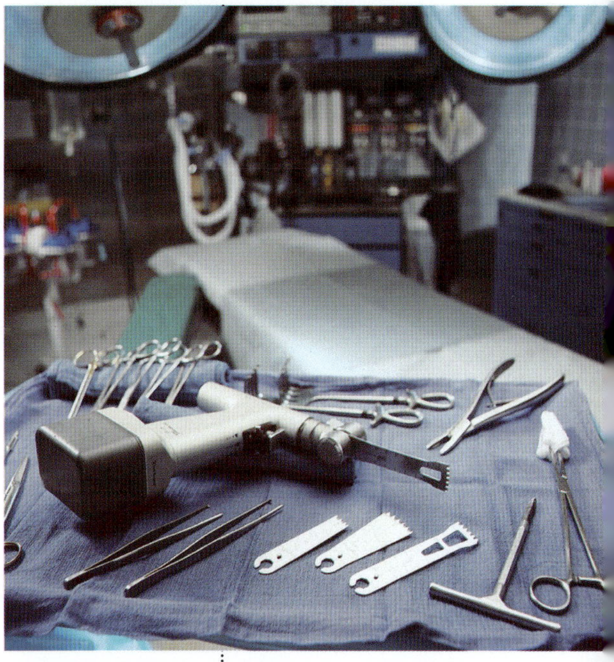

Being a solution provider in the industry is of the utmost importance to Brasseler USA. This is evidenced by the fact that Brasseler USA representatives are present in all dental schools and helps to fund student scholarships. Its highly educated direct sales force of over 100 professionals, supported by a technical and customer service staff, work with clinicians on a daily basis to satisfy their rotary cutting instrument needs. Customers can also find Brasseler USA on the World Wide Web at www.brasselerusa.com for assistance with techniques, product selection, and new product information.

Excelling in the production of dental rotary instruments is just one area of pride, according to Waters. The creation of Komet Medical Surgical Power Accessories in 1987 affirmed the company's commitment to the precision and quality of its broad rotary cutting instrument product line. Using research engineers and consulting physicians, Komet Medical developed a line of surgical power accessories including both rotary cutters and surgical saw blades for use by orthopedic surgeons, neurosurgeons, otolaryngologists (ENT surgeons), cardio-vascular surgeons, and other physicians. The Komet Medical product line also includes batteries for power systems, battery testers, battery chargers, and high-speed motor drill systems. Komet Medical's customers are located in markets throughout the world.

■ Komet Medical is committed to the precision and quality of its broad cutting instrument product line.

Brasseler USA continues to diversify. In 1995, the Company assigned a staff of research and development and sales personnel to develop products specifically for the aerospace industry. These specialty tools provide quick, smooth, aggressive cutting of all types of alloys. This team of experts design products for the industry's manufacturing needs including tools for the rebuilding of jet turbines and engines.

As a community leader in the support of charity, Brasseler USA has become one of Savannah's finest corporate citizens. The company helps to support the United Way, American Cancer Society, and Ronald McDonald House Charities as well as sponsors a company blood drive every year. Brasseler USA sponsors many community business events including the recent opening of the International Trade and Convention Center and the Savannah Area Chamber of Commerce Annual Campaign. However, Brasseler USA's principal charitable activity is the support of dental and medical education. Through its innovative Brasseler Scholars Program, the company sponsors an annual competition to select the leading dental student in the area of aesthetic dentistry from the class of rising seniors at every dental school in the United States (and soon, Canada). From these finalists a panel of leading educators selects two to five Brasseler Scholars. In addition, the company has sponsored dental school professorships.

The future looks very promising for Brasseler USA. The dental industry is growing and expected to double over the next several years. Brasseler USA is heavily involved in working with leading clinicians in order to remain an innovative solution provider. The medical division has tremendous domestic and international growth opportunity for large and small bone power as well as in the fields of otolaryngology surgery, orthopedic surgery, and neurosurgery. Savannah's manufacturing and distribution facility continues to grow in order to meet the needs of the company and the markets it serves.

■ Brasseler USA is headquartered in a modern 85,000-square-foot facility.

EM Industries

"Nearly 50 percent of our employees have been here ten years or longer and we are proud of it."

From the finest automobiles to the most vivid wall coverings and packaging, the world shimmers thanks to the efforts of one Savannah industry. Employing a staff of more than 150 scientists, manufacturing and office personnel, EM Industries, Inc. brought its myriad of skills to Savannah in 1979 as a pearl pigment production facility, manufacturing effect pigments for automotive, industrial, and cosmetic applications. Today, resulting from a strong commitment to research and development and dedicated to innovation in all business fields, EM Industries maintains a prominent reputation as a progressive company.

■ The EM Industries Team in Savannah produces effect pigments and evaporation chemicals for an international market.

Strategically located in the heart of the southeastern United States, the impressive Savannah plant is part of EM Industries' Chemicals and Pigments Division headquartered in Hawthorne, New York. The company is the United States' affiliate of Merck KGaA, Darmstadt, Germany, an international pharmaceutical, specialty chemical laboratory products company that boasts a widely recognized name.

The success of EM Industries has evolved through years of growth and is based on rather humble beginnings. Founded in 1668 as a small pharmacy with the name "Angel" by Emanuel Merck (the company's inspiration for its "EM" title), the Merck KGaA Group today represents a global organization with annual sales of more than $4 billion. Its 33,000 employees are spread over 171 separate companies in 48 countries worldwide. Hence, the company that celebrated its beginnings as a small pharmacy now runs its manufacturing operations in 25 countries at 63 different locations. With more than $4 million dedicated to research and development, the Merck KGaA Group is consistently proving its technological superiority, providing innovation in all of its business fields.

■ In our car paints, printing inks, cosmetics, and many other fields you will find EM Industries' pearl pigments.

While the larger part of the Merck KGaA business takes place in Europe, the United States market represents approximately 24 percent of worldwide sales. Founded in the United States in 1970, EM Industries is represented in North America at 13 locations and three production sites: Savannah, Georgia; Norwood, Ohio; and Gibbstown, New Jersey. The Norwood facility manufactures high-purity solvents and reagents while the Gibbstown location manufactures reagents and diagnostic products. Together, these two facilities form EM Science, the laboratory division of EM Industries. With names like CN Biosciences, Dey, Genpharm, VWR, Lexigen and Lipha, all group-owned companies, EM Industries represents the U.S. part of Merck KGaA Darmstadt, Germany.

The Canadian market is covered by BDH in Toronto, which is a mirror image of EM Industries in its business segments and customers. Both EM Science and BDH handle a large part of their business through the EM Industries' laboratory supply company, VWR Scientific Products Corporation, based in West Chester, Pennsylvania.

The EM Industries' product portfolio consists of more than 20,000 products that are widely popular in a variety of products today. They include pharmaceuticals and vitamins, separation media and reagents, laboratory supplies and electronic chemicals, liquid crystals, effect pigments, and evaporation chemicals, to name a few.

■ MODERN EQUIPMENT IS NECESSARY TO GUARANTEE STABLE PIGMENT QUALITY FOR THE WHOLE LIFETIME OF THE PRODUCT.

THE EVOLUTION OF THE SAVANNAH PLANT

The need to build a manufacturing plant for the effect pigments and evaporation chemicals led to the foundation and growth of the Savannah location. In November 1979, the groundwork was laid for this fast-growing and successful production site. The first to operate on the Savannah premises was the Mica Pigment Production Plant, and ever since that plant was dedicated, it has continued to prosper.

Based on the city's proximity to highway, rail, air, and sea transportation resources, Savannah was the perfect site for the company's location, according to its vice president of operations, Dr. Bernhard Mainz. Situated near major interstates, the Savannah harbor with access to the Savannah River and the Atlantic Ocean, and the Savannah International Airport, this location links EM Industries to the world. When it opened, the Savannah plant was the group's second mica pigment production site in the world after Gernsheim, Germany. Today, another production plant in Onahama, Japan has become a part of the International Pigment Production Team of Merck KGaA, Darmstadt, Germany.

Savannah, a city that is famous for its picturesque historic district and fine architecture, is also a leader in products that are recognized worldwide, a fact known to few. Marketed under the trade name Affair, the pigments manufactured in Savannah for automotive and industrial purposes are non-toxic, metal oxide-coated mica flakes that are used in a variety of products, including automobile paints, printing inks, packaging materials and wall coverings. These pigments give the host material, such

■ EFFICIENT QUALITY CONTROL AND RESEARCH FACILITIES ARE THE BASIS FOR THE PRODUCT QUALITY TODAY AND TOMORROW.

as plastic, paint or ink, a shimmery, lustrous quality, even in very low concentrations. A gold pigment produced in Savannah is used in Germany's paper currency to discourage counterfeiting. Mica-based pigments are also produced specifically for cosmetic applications and are used in numerous products such as eye shadows, lipsticks, and nail lacquers.

Through the years, several production expansions were necessary to fulfill the fast growing market requirements. The biggest single step took place in 1987 when the production capacity in Savannah was doubled. The second operation on the EM Industries site in Savannah was the production for Patinals—EM Industries' brand for evaporation chemicals.

Like the mica pigments, these products are present in many areas of our everyday lives. Anti-reflective coatings on lenses for cameras, projectors, and eyeglasses are unthinkable without modern evaporation chemicals. These light-controlling substances subdue light and keep reflections to a minimum to improve the optical qualities of all kinds of optical instruments. Liquid crystal monitors for laptops and cameras feature brilliant colors and bright light due to the transparent conductive coatings, which are possible with products like Patinals. One of the Patinal substances serves as a raw material in the industry for counterfeit safe special pigments; it actually appears on the U.S. paper currency. Starting within the mica building in 1981, the Patinal growth led to its own dedicated production building in 1990. The Patinal product line is also produced in Gernsheim, Germany.

The preparation of mica based pearl luster pigments was started in Savannah in 1979.

To serve the vast U.S. market with customized products, and to support research activities in Germany, EM Industries founded its own Mica Pigments Research and Development Department in Savannah in 1988. The first research and development activities were located in a combined administration/laboratories building. It soon became necessary to provide more resources and space for these activities; therefore, in 1991, the R&D Department moved into its own building.

In 1995, the Savannah site got its last big production addition. A production plant for Bismuth-based pearl pigments completed the overall manufacturing activities in Savannah. Everyday products such as buttons and greeting cards, as well as cosmetics, provide opportunities for these unique lustrous finishes. Particularly interesting is the environmentally friendly effect of these pigments. In the past, pigments containing lead have been used to achieve the shiny pearl effect in buttons. Now, Bismuth-based pigments, free of any toxic heavy metals, may be used to create its same wonderful effect. Imbedded in the material of medical catheters, Bismuth pigments help surgeons easily locate catheters in the human body, as the pigment is highly visible in x-ray pictures.

The Bismuth R&D team joined the Mica R&D team in the same building located within the Savannah site. The R&D Departments in Savannah, Germany, and Japan together form an internationally coordinated research force to provide the world market with high quality and innovative products. The proximity of the R &D facilities to the production plants led to fast and smooth transfers of the newest Research and Development results into production and, of course, into the market.

The preparation of customized shiny Bismuth Oxychloride Crystals is even today still an art and a well kept secret.

EM Industries' reputation for high quality products and service is one of many reasons the company continues its successful presence in the industry. Whether technical support for special effect pigments such as the Mica pigments or the Bismuth-based pearl pigments, customers continue to count on EM as their total resource supplier. Ongoing technical support to resolve pigment settling in nail lacquers and shampoos, for the protection of abrasion in spray nozzles, the agglomeration of pigment particles in paints or to find the right formulation for an eye shadow is readily available. The Applications Technical Laboratories resolve these technical concerns. Savannah houses Applications Technical Laboratories for Pigment Applications in plastics, printing inks, powder coatings, and automotive paints and coatings. An Applications Technical Laboratory for all cosmetic applications is located at the EM Industries Headquarters in Hawthorne, New York.

Patinal products are used for optical systems and security printing.

The three production plants along with the departments for human resources, engineering and maintenance, quality assurance, cost accounting and purchasing, safety/health and environment, quality control, warehousing and local network administration, comprise EM Industries' Savannah site.

"Our biggest assets," Dr. Bernhard Mainz, vice president of operations, says, "are the established and experienced employees here in Savannah. Many of them have been here since the plant was built in 1979. Nearly 50 percent of our employees have been here ten years or longer and we are proud of it. With this seasoned team, EM Industries represents a modern, customer-oriented company possessing the important tools to serve an international market."

The development of new color effects is an interesting and always new challenge.

InterMarine Savannah

Among its most positive attributes are the facility's access to the Atlantic Ocean.

136' Mia Elise cruising the Savannah River in front of the "Waving Girl" statue.

The golden cast shed by the late afternoon sun along Savannah's historic riverfront now has a new sparkle. For just a few hundred feet down from the pubs, restaurants, and shops that give Savannah her charm, an old industrial shipyard is glistening with sleek mega-yachts. Employees who once constructed mine sweepers for the U.S. Navy are now inspired and practicing their skills on gleaming luxury vessels. Indeed, to the delight of economic forecasters and lovers of the sea, the marriage of history and yachting has led to a new look along this rustic, old slice of land that once endured the hardships of World War II.

With a 20-year veteran of the boat-building business at its helm and a group of Fortune 100 investors in the foreground, InterMarine Savannah is fast becoming one of the world's most highly acclaimed places to bring yachts more than a hundred feet in length for repair and maintenance. But servicing yachts is just one task performed at InterMarine Savannah. This company is also in the construction business—boldly entering the market of yachts built on spec for consumers who want to sail without enduring a lengthy building process. With 95-, 118-, 120-, 145- and 123-footers under construction—InterMarine Savannah's new marketing strategy yields costs-savings that are pleasing to the consumer.

"A consumer can pull up to our facility, select their colors (without changing the general design) and pull away from our shipyard for less time it would take to construct a custom-built vessel," said Patta Sloan Conboy, InterMarine Savannah's marketing director.

Surprised? Don't be. Thomas Conboy, InterMarine Savannah's chief operating officer says the changes along the riverfront are simply a sign of the times.

"The megayacht industry has changed," he said. "There was a day when requests for custom yachts that took two or more years to build were prevalent. Today, the common denominator is timing. Most of our customers have busy schedules and lifestyles and they want a yacht now. We're looking to deliver three to four boats a year and we are building our yachts to a very high level of quality."

158' Feadship Mi Gaea in the 535' long graving dock with cover.

It is that level of quality that is attracting customers to the Savannah-based company. Here, they can partake of the ambiance of the city filled with splendid architecture and fine cuisine; delight in a spirited nightlife, and be lured to natural beauty of the beach and waterways of Savannah while overseeing construction or selecting fabrics and fine surfaces in InterMarine's tidy production facility.

Among its most positive attributes are the facility's access to the Atlantic Ocean. The 21-acre shipyard is located just 20 miles from the ocean up the Savannah River. Like the massive freighters it hosts, the river accommodates depths up to 40 feet (mean controlling depth). The scenic channel provides bluewater access to everything from pleasure craft to 1000-foot container ships, and the yard itself is less than a 5-minute drive from the historic downtown.

Designed as a yard specifically to build minesweepers and submarine rescue ships for the U.S. Navy from 1941 until 1947, InterMarine's skilled labor force became highly respected for its superior construction skills. In 1986, InterMarine USA was born, and soon became world-famous for establishing designing and constructing reinforced plastic minehunters for the Navy. With goals to construct 188-foot battle ready fiberglass minehunters with hulls nearly six inches thick, the company became the foremost expert in the construction of very large, composite hulls. To accommodate Navy contracts, InterMarine developed the expansive Savannah facility capable of handling heavy tonnage and today, that centerpiece is the yard's 535- by 73-foot graving dock that is nearly as long as two football fields joined end-to-end.

Capable of tenderly handling today's luxury yachts, this graving dock is unlike traditional dry docks which sink and then raise a vessel clear out of the water. Instead, it is more like a lock system. Vessels with as much as a 21-foot draft are floated into the dock, then the riverfront opening is closed and the dock pumped dry. A 360-foot long retractable shed is in place, making InterMarine Savannah the "largest boat house in North America" boasting the largest cover of its kind.

In addition, the yard has a level-platform railway capable of hauling vessels 200 feet in length and weighing 1,000 tons. InterMarine Savannah utilizes this unique railway to haul megayachts and then side-shift them onto a concrete pad for outdoor work. A 160,000 square foot shed is used for retrofit and repair work on large vessels and serves as a production facility for the company's new line of spec yachts.

118' INTERMARINE "SAVANNAH" SHOT ON LOCATION IN DOWNTOWN SAVANNAH IS THE MOST RECENT YACHT DELIVERED.

THE INTERIOR DINING HALL IS AS ELEGANT AS THE EXTERIOR OF EACH AND EVERY YACHT BUILT AT INTERMARINE SAVANNAH.

InterMarine's first test of megayacht construction came in 1996 with an ABS inspected and classed, 111-foot custom vessel. The second, Mia Elise, a 136-foot motor yacht, was successfully delivered, as has the third, The Waving Girl, a 105-foot yacht named for a Savannah landmark and completed in 1999. Launched from the Savannah yard, The Waving Girl left behind a yard filled with vessels ranging in length from 147-feet to a 300-footer, all in for repair and maintenance—a sure sign of the company's newfound success. Boasting a safe environment and a highly skilled work force, InterMarine Savannah's full-service facility boasts on-site tradesmen skilled in joinery, metal work, bottom/top-coat paint systems, and machinists and fitters certified in ABS and Lloyds classification. "InterMarine is steadfast in setting and meeting accurate timetables, thereby allowing customers the opportunity to enjoy their yachts," said Conboy.

It is the energetic vision of the owners; the skill of more than 320 employees; the proximity to the ocean; and the flavor of a resort-like hub that is attracting yachts and owners from all over the world to Savannah's shores. And now, the city's acclaimed reputation as having the country's largest historic district is now complimented by the fine art of building and repairing megayachts.

Southern Exposure

Business, Finance & The Professions

Maggie Van Wie

Savannah Area Chamber of Commerce

The city's flare for hospitality has resulted in tourism industry milestones in the Savannah and Chatham County area.

■ The Historic Savannah RiverFront at dusk comes alive with city lights.

On the heels of a best-selling novel; after hosting more than 40 major motion pictures and hundreds of colorful festivals and world-class athletic events, Savannah has become one of the hottest destinations in the country. America's first planned city has relished her reputation as a lavishly dressed lady adorned in architectural brilliance and drenched in year-round blossoms. But with ingenious community leadership, she has aged with grace and energy to attract a new league of guests. Literally thousands of athletes and families have flocked to the city for swim meets in a state-of-the-art natatorium; soccer matches on an expansive, new playing field; and weightlifting competitions in a world-class training facility. They've sampled the waters of the nearby Atlantic Ocean where a yearly kingfish tournament that has challenged fishermen from all over the country. The supporting ecosystem with its thick with marsh grass, winding salt-marsh creeks, and a beautiful beach perched beside the Atlantic Ocean has brought nature lovers to discover a land that attracted its first settlers more than 200 years ago. Hence, the city that once drew visitors to her shores to explore the gardens and homes of the nation's largest historic district is now appealing to the masses with a diverse menu of events and activities.

■ This centuries old fountain has always been a favorite attraction for the millions of Savannah visitors each year.

Word of the city's energetic persona is spreading thanks to those who have dined in some of the country's most heralded restaurants and eateries and hopped aboard trolleys for tours. Not only is Savannah attracting a year-round audience comprised of all age groups, but the city's reputation for being a fun place to compete, visit, and live is spreading and those who have already sampled Savannah are coming back for more. They've discovered Savannah's 21 pristine, live-oak covered squares, toured magnificent homes and even shopped in 18th century galleries, quaint antique shops, intimate pubs, and even 20th century malls. When nighttime falls, guests have enjoyed the city's array of accommodations as they've stayed in more than 9,000 rooms ranging from the most intimate and nostalgic bed and breakfasts to the most modern and luxurious hotels.

It's no wonder *Forbes* magazine named Savannah as one of its top 200 "Best Places" in the country for the year 2000.

Savannah is an easy sell. The sheer brilliance of its eclectic architecture (created by master architects hired by wealthy cotton merchants in the 1800s); its mild climate (ranging from 51 degrees in winter to 66 degrees in spring and 88 degrees in summer); and its lush, tropical landscaping makes it the perfect year-round destination. It's so perfect, that, in fact, *The New York Times* named Savannah as one of its "Top 12 Trendy Hot Spots in the World," in 1999. Other publications, including *Conde Nast Traveler*, included Savannah in its "Top 10 U.S. Cities to Visit," also in 1999, and *Family Fun* cited the city as one of the "Top 10 Southeast Cities for Family Vacations."

The city's flare for hospitality has resulted in tourism industry milestones in the Savannah and Chatham County area. With tourism as the area's largest employer, the SACVB's contributions to the area's economy are vital to the community's continued prosperity. Visitors in 1998 alone stayed a total of 10.7 million days and spent $1.1 billion.

Additionally, new facilities are creating a market for tourists that run year-round as opposed to seasonal. The $83 million Savannah International Maritime Trade and Convention Center, replete with highly advanced multi-media technology, opened its doors to rave reviews from its first conventioneers.

"In the final analysis, the excellent service your community provided our group is the main reason we intend to return to this great city," said Wendy Cantwell, event director of the Ashphalt Conference and Expo (the first event director to utilize the new facilities). The trade center, along with its resplendent new neighbor, The Westin Harbor Savannah Resort, and The Club at Savannah Harbor, have brought new life to the land across the river. That modern $98 million five-star resort boasts nearly 400-rooms and a world-recognized Greenbrier spa. Adding to the nautical atmosphere of the riverfront are colorful water ferries that empty out onto Savannah's shoreline where more than 9,000 hotel and motel rooms await. Meeting space averaging 10,000 square feet in each of the city's five major hotels and an additional 330,000 square feet of exhibit halls, ballrooms, and smaller meeting rooms at the convention center are splashed with Savannah's style and color.

THIS MAJESTIC HISTORIC MANSION IS ONE OF MANY TURN OF THE CENTURY HOMES THAT LINE SAVANNAH'S GASTON STREET.

The persistence and dedication of the Savannah Area Convention and Visitors Bureau staff and board has paid off. In 1999, their efforts to market the city produced 160 meetings and convention contracts with projected revenues of $18 million. Those numbers include 575 tour contracts with projected revenues of $1.75 million and include more than 200 print articles and hours of television and radio coverage. In addition, the Bureau's media relations department hosted more than 130 visits from 150 writers and had contact with 400 writers, editors, or publications. The department representatives attended three regional and national writers meetings to promote the city and assisted with television shoots for U.S., Canadian, British, Irish, and German networks. A new partnership with American Express resulted in a direct-mail campaign that put Savannah travel planners in the mailboxes of 150,000 southeast residents and 5,000 travel agencies. The investment in advertising to promote Savannah rose almost 400 percent last year.

Savannah Area Convention and Visitors Bureau leaders are glancing toward the future with eagerness and bracing for an explosion in tourism

Visiting the city now is a mere tap away. A modern website (www.savannahvisit.com) not only takes inquisitive guests on a pictorial tour of the city, but links users with hotels, motels, inns, restaurants, shops, and galleries. More than 2,000 people visit there each day and as a result, often visit the city to partake of its splendor and hospitality. As a festival city, exciting events are offered throughout the year and range from the Savannah Onstage International Arts Festival to the second largest St. Patrick's Day parade when half a million people flock to her shores for the celebration.

The charm of the city seems to keep growing. Almost weekly, the city takes center stage in top publications from all over the world. In fact, the city was named "One of the Top 10 Walking Cities," by *Walking Magazine* and "The Most Beautiful City in North America," by *LeMonde* of Paris, France. *Outlook*, a trade publication, lists the port city as one of the top 25 places in the country to live and work. And in March, the city was named "One of the Top 10 Places to Watch a St. Patrick's Day Parade," by *USA Today*, who also named one of Savannah's restaurants as "the best place to eat " in 1999.

Whether it's the array of beautiful photographs from the city's web page or a feature-length film that attracts the visitor to Savannah, it is the city's people who extend the warmth and grace of true Southern hospitality to its guests and keeps them coming back for more.

TYBEE ISLAND, JUST 20 MINUTES FROM HISTORIC DOWNTOWN SAVANNAH, IS A HAVEN FOR THOSE SEEKING A COASTAL PERSPECTIVE.

Darby Bank and Trust Company

Darby Bank is fast becoming one of Savannah's greatest banking resources.

■ Darby Bank offers its customers the knowledge and expertise of a larger bank but with small-town, friendly customer service.

In an age where big institutions are primarily banking on technology for success, a small-town bank is making big-city strides using a personal, friendly approach to business.

In 1995, Darby Bank and Trust Company of Vidalia bet on success by taking a unique approach to its marketing tactics. First, the Bank's founders, realizing the need for change, looked to a Savannah professional for leadership. They landed Walter Bowden, a prominent and highly respected Savannahian whose passion is banking and whose affection has been small communities—a Savannahian whose career began with the old Savannah Bank and Trust.

Bowden, following his instincts, bet that the personal touch exhibited by small community banks would work in a city ruled by nationally prominent banks. Acknowledging that headquarters would remain in Vidalia, Bowden placed his trust in small businesses eager for growth. While big-city banks often place branches in smaller cities, this rural bank opted to reverse the strategy and open a branch in Savannah.

Darby Bank began making its sweep across the Savannah community. Today, signs of its prominence are spread from the city's Southside to the Historic District.

The story of Darby Bank's success is indeed singular.

The Start of a Banking Phenomenon

Darby Bank & Trust Company opened its doors on May 28, 1927 as the J.F. Darby Bank, started by J. Frank Darby. A popular meeting place for its townspeople, trust and respect for this family-run operation spread. On June 22, 1934, the Bank was incorporated under the name of Darby Banking Co. and became a state-chartered bank. James F. Darby, Jr. ran the Bank between 1948 and 1991. In 1989, a holding company was formed serving Toombs, Chatham, and surrounding areas. DBT Holding Company became the parent for Darby Bank and Trust.

■ Salita R. Hill, Senior Vice President, Walter B. Bowden, President/CEO of DBT Holding Company, and Connie D. Williams, Chair of DBT Holding Company.

It wasn't until 1997 that the trusted small-town bank began to make an entrance in one of Georgia's fastest growing cities, Savannah. That is when the President of DBT Holding Co. of Vidalia, Walter Bowden, faced strong loan demand after opening a branch in Savannah. Without enough core deposits to fund those loans, a DB&T Vice President, John A. Tyson, approached Bowden with an interesting proposition. Tyson's research uncovered deposits from across the nation, money available from deposit brokers and from electronic bulletin boards that bring buyers and sellers of deposits together without a middleman. Today, the DBT Holding Company, parent company of Darby Bank and Trust Company, generates about 40 percent of its funding from deposits collected from outside its Georgia market.

At the close of 1999, the Bank's officers had reason to celebrate. Net income at the Holding Company increased by 21.4 percent and total assets grew by 35.5 percent. The Bank's return on equity for the Holding Company was 12.3 percent and as overhead increased, the loan loss reserve grew from $260,000 in 1995 to $2,059,000 on December 31, 1999 with $607,000 added in 1999 alone.

"Savannah was a logical expansion market for Darby Bank because of my contacts and the connections of our board of directors as well as the fact that Connie Williams, the daughter of the founder, lived there. We were looking for a new market because

Toombs County had seven banks, six of which were locally owned. It is difficult to expand in a market that size which has only 24,000 people. So, we looked at Savannah. We have made an effort to go out and initially do business with people that we know to get a good, solid base for business without the risk of dealing with unknown quantities," says Bowden.

"I think the small community bank has a permanent place, even if consolidations continue and the overall number of banking companies continues to shrink. But it is going to be critical that they be run more efficiently and be sound credit-wise and technology-wise. You are not going to survive unless you are a small, well-run institution," he added. Competing with giants is no easy task, but, according to Bowden, Darby Bank's unique approach to banking is the key to the Bank's future.

■ The Savannah Officer Group—Standing left to right: David R. Graham, Jacqueline D. Fall, Brenda C. Wheeles, Hope C. Fuller, Linda J. Key, and P. Brad Hunnings. Seated left to right: Susan C. Getty and Salita R. Hill.

Bowden now resides in Vidalia and travels to and from the Bank's Vidalia home-office as needed. He enjoys interacting with his former banking customers in Savannah many of whom are now Darby's greatest fans. Bowden's visions for a prospering future for this community bank in Savannah are starting to pay off. To a newcomer driving through the streets of Savannah, Darby's presence is evident by modest green and white signs that adorn properties under restoration or construction. To the local businessperson, Darby Bank's one-on-one approach to lending has been a key ingredient in making dreams come true. When the first Savannah branch opened several years ago, Savannah's historical buildings and sluggish streets suddenly began to emerge into an overgrowth of new renovation and construction. Today, with little or no advertising, except by word-of-mouth, Darby Bank is fast becoming one of Savannah's greatest banking resources.

"I'm thrilled with the personal service and quick answers I get from the staff at Darby Bank," says Rob Sales, co-owner of The Magnolia Place Inn. "Savannah is fortunate to have a banking presence that hasn't forgotten about good, old-fashioned, face-to-face customer service."

"What we will have to sell is the value of our relationship with small businesses and small-business people," Bowden says. In part, Darby Bank's success is due to the fact that many of the Bank's employees have come from larger institutions. They bring a strong sense of family to the Bank as well as the experience of working with customers in a one-on-one atmosphere.

"Our employees are just like our customers, they long for that personal touch," he says. Bowden praises Darby Bank employees for keeping customers satisfied and loyal and displays optimism for the Bank's future in Georgia.

"Neither the Internet nor big institutions (bank or non-banks) can properly handle the requirements of a small business-person who needs someone to listen and care about their business. Consequently, we feel that our niche will allow us to continue to grow and prosper in the midst of upheaval within our industry."

■ Darby Bank Board of Directors—Front row left to right: Walter B. Bowden, Donald H. Estroff, Helen T. Darby, Connie D. Williams, and J. Edward Tyson. Standing left to right: G. Larry Threlkeld, Royce J. Palmer, Richard D. Williams, William E. Bedingfield, Richard Platt, W. Emory Davis, R.H. DeJarnette, Jr., Reid Threlkeld, and S. Wayne Smith.

Pitney Bowes

Pitney Bowes is now a vital part of the Savannah community and is nearly 300 employees strong.

One man's dream to handle the mail more efficiently led to an industrial feat that changed history, and today, that man's philosophy is still reaching customers worldwide from offices all over the country, including a lakeside setting in Savannah, Georgia.

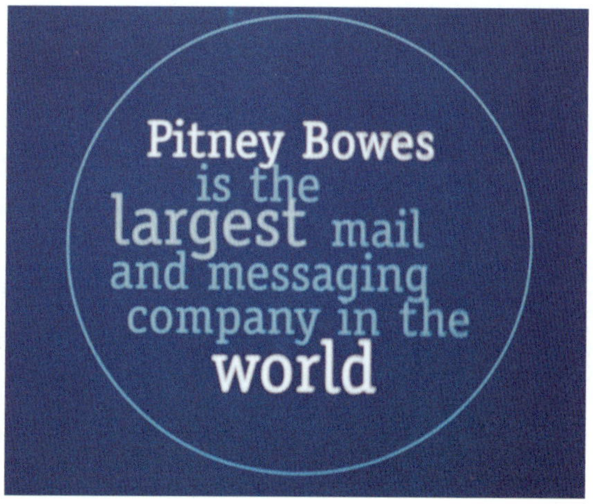

■ "People friendly, product smart."

Pitney Bowes, the company that first introduced the postage meter to the world, is now a vital part of the Savannah community and is nearly 300 employees strong. The company's Office Direct Division customer contact center located to the city in 1998 and today offers Savannahians who work there a "whole life experience." Jan Carpenter, director of operations of the Savannah Call Center, said, "Savannah's Pitney Bowes' employees boast skills and enthusiasm for duties that reach customers nationally. Basically, we're proud to have such an enthusiastic group of employees. In essence, we have a work force that likes their jobs," he said.

Precisely, Savannah's center assists small business customers with billing, meter leases, servicing existing customers, and out-bounding to non-customers. More than 90 percent of its employees are from the Savannah/Chatham County area and those numbers continue to grow. "Savannah was simply the right choice," said Carpenter. "Our efforts were to locate to a city with the right workforce, and we've got that here." With technology so amazing that postage can now be transmitted through the Internet, Pitney Bowes continues to relish its intriguing past. In the early 1920s, a Chicago, Illinois, clerk bored with his job, entertained himself with new inventions and by the turn of the century, he was experimenting with ways of sticking postage stamps on letters with the help of a newly devised machine. Arthur Hill Pitney concluded that a machine that could actually print stamps right on the envelope would do away with the costly and time-consuming process of buying, licking, and sticking.

On October 14, 1902, a patent was granted and Pitney started a company called the Pitney Postal Machine Company, which in 1910, became the American Postage Meter Company. Nine years later, Pitney received

■ The Personal Post™ meter and accompanying 5 lb scale. This is the first postage meter created and priced specifically to meet the needs of small offices.

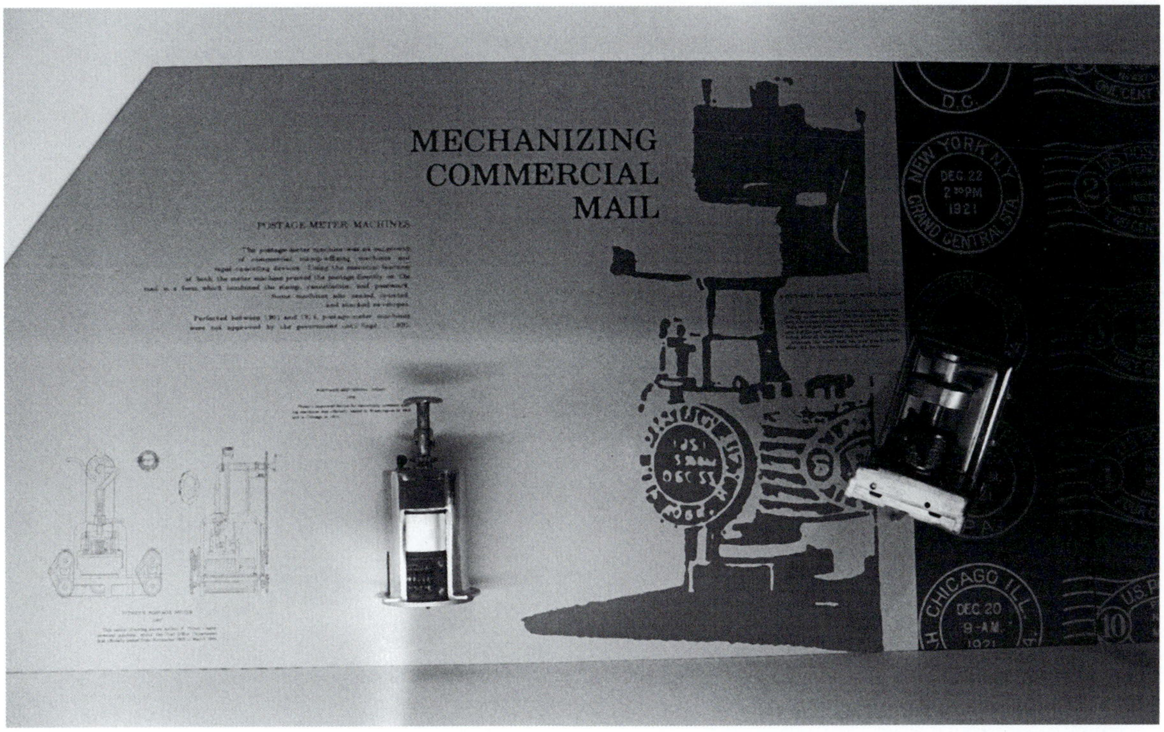

■ ONE OF PITNEY'S EARLY POSTAGE METERS. THE PRINTING MECHANISM AND TOTAL REGISTER WERE ENCLOSED IN AN INACCESSIBLE METAL CASING, TO BE OPENED ONLY AT THE POST OFFICE.

an invitation from Walter Harold Bowes, an English-born entrepreneur who owned the Universal Stamping Machine Company in Stamford, Connecticut, to become a team and achieve an even more productive product.

Pitney and Bowes soon began work on a machine for mailing that did not use stamps and soon a new company was born—the Pitney Bowes Postage Meter Company. (When the two inventors met up with a mechanically gifted man named Walter Heber Wheeler, Jr., a faulty clutch backstop in the new postage meter was repaired, impressing and acquiring the support of the United States Post Office.)

From those days of early success, the company has reached new heights in the industry, today becoming a $4.4 billion global provider of informed mail and messaging management. Recently named as *Business Ethics Magazine*'s List of The 100 Best Corporate Citizens, the company was recognized for its profitability and exceeding its social responsibilities for employees, customers, community members, and stockholders.

Although it received high marks in Customer Relations and Employee Relations, Pitney Bowes was selected for its targeted commitment to the community. Those company strengths are indeed evident in Savannah. "Our employees are proud to support the community through efforts like Learning for Life, a series of career skills workshops conducted for high school students," said Carpenter. "Savannah is not only a great place to live, but it provides some wonderful opportunities for community involvement."

Volunteerism has also been a cornerstone in Pitney Bowes' community efforts. In 1997, Pitney Bowes began a formal employee volunteer program called PB People: Building Stronger Communities. Currently, over 250 employees from Pitney Bowes have donated over 1800 hours to 22 projects. Their efforts focus on such areas as education, human services, and community improvement projects.

What's in store for Pitney Bowes during the next century? According to the company's corporate profile, three industry segments: mailing and integrated logistics, office solutions, and capital services will continue to meet the demands of today's customers. And from the Savannah workforce, that means making the customer's job easier.

"We're going to continue to make sure our customers understand that we care about them. We want to convey to them that their satisfaction is the most important job we have," Carpenter concluded.

■ A FRONT VIEW OF THE CALL CENTER.

Hunter, Maclean, Exley & Dunn, P.C.

With more than 50 attorneys, Hunter Maclean offers one comprehensive source to handle the full range of each client's legal needs.

■ For over 100 years, Hunter Maclean has been committed to serving its clients and has been connected to its community. Pictured left to right: Brooks Stillwell and Bobby Glenn.

Hunter, Maclean, Exley & Dunn, P.C. is the largest law firm in the state of Georgia outside of Atlanta. The firm maintains its principal office in Savannah, the center of a booming coastal region. It also maintains offices in Atlanta and Augusta. Hunter Maclean represents a wide variety of companies and individuals throughout Georgia, the Southeast, and the United States in their legal and business matters in Georgia. Hunter Maclean is a law firm that is committed to its clients, and connected to the communities in which its clients do business.

The firm has extensive experience representing businesses and individuals. Its clients include Fortune 500 manufacturing companies, locally-based small businesses, banks and hospitals, professional service organizations, a school board, an industrial development authority, and nonprofit corporations.

With more than 50 attorneys, Hunter Maclean offers one comprehensive source to handle the full range of each client's legal needs. The firm is organized into "practice areas," which include legal services applicable to most businesses, such as tax and employment law and business litigation, as well as specialized legal services for specific industries.

These practice areas include bankruptcy/work-outs, business organization, employee benefits, estate planning/probate, immigration, insurance law, intellectual property, products liability, litigation, taxation, toxic torts, and zoning/land use. Commercial practice areas also include finance, leasing, and securities.

Industry-specific practice areas include health care, hotel/hospitality, construction, real estate (residential and development), banking, environmental, schools, admiralty, medical malpractice defense, transportation, and industrial development.

■ John Tatum, attorney at law with Hunter Maclean, demonstrates a motto the firm practices daily. "We believe in listening to our clients."

To ensure advantageous and long-standing working relationships with its clients, Hunter Maclean encourages frequent communication with clients on planning and implementing their business or litigation strategies. The firm also encourages frank discussion and agreement with its clients on performance objectives, staffing requirements, and billing arrangements. The firm employs state-of-the-art technology that enables it to work effectively and efficiently on any transaction or case.

These progressive attitudes and practices contribute to Hunter Maclean's ability to attract key talent as they continue to grow the law firm with experienced legal professionals in all three city offices.

Hunter Maclean's attorneys are involved in many community activities. They frequently serve on governmental boards and commissions, and are active in social service and arts organizations throughout Georgia. The firm represents over a dozen nonprofit organizations on a pro bono basis. Hunter Maclean is committed to serving its clients, and its communities, and to helping generate the long-term prosperity of both.

Bailey Davidson

Real Estate, Development & Construction

Jie Yu

Cora Bett Thomas Realty

Cora Bett Thomas' professional career in Savannah has spanned 30 years.

■ Cora Bett Thomas.

Gracious Southern receptions filled with the warmth and color of historic Savannah come naturally to Cora Bett Thomas. Filled with pride for her city, the president and owner of Cora Bett Thomas Realty welcomes real estate inquiries with enthusiasm and charm.

"Savannah is not just a place to live, it is a way of living. It is our distinct pleasure to graciously introduce newcomers to our wonderful community. We do look forward to meeting all who choose to sample our city," she said.

Focused on Savannah's Historic District since 1975, Cora Bett Thomas is recognized as the area's leader in representing not only the district's elegant antebellum mansions and finest town homes, but also residential and gated communities throughout Savannah. The Victorian District, Ardsley Park, various island communities including Tybee Island, Wilmington, The Landings at Skidaway and Hutchinson Island—Savannah's newest residential golf resort—bear her company's name, as do deepwater intercoastal waterfront locations, exciting oceanfront properties, estates and plantations located in the lowcountry of South Carolina and Georgia. Cora Bett Thomas Realty's services extend to the complete range of commercial investment opportunities and a full service property management and rental division.

■ City Hall Dome.

Flanked by live oaks, tropical foliage and historic architecture, the company's newly renovated facility boasts an invitingly upscale facade and is situated in the heart of the Historic District. Equipped with the latest in computer technology, Cora Bett Thomas Realty is managed by a highly skilled and licensed core of expert sales associates and support staff. Additionally, the agency provides an unsurpassed level of personalized client service marked by the firm's established standards of confidentiality, discretion, and reliability.

Cora Bett Thomas' professional career in Savannah has spanned 30 years. In 1970 when she left her home state of North Carolina, she never dreamed that one day real estate signs bearing her name would grace the lawns of the South's most magnificent historic residences and the coastline's most gracious island homes. Enticed by Savannah's splendid architecture and aesthetic setting, Thomas developed a passion for the city's Historic District and soon purchased and renovated several properties. Living among the picturesque homes and beautiful squares prompted her to begin buying and selling properties, and she soon became a licensed real estate agent. Her talents led to several years as a multi-million-dollar producer, and over the next 20 years she established her reputation as the premier agent and broker in the area. Commenting on the challenges of the real estate business, she noted, "The key is to have the intuitive ability to appreciate the needs of both buyer and seller. Our team accomplishes this by conveying a blend of professional expertise in a harmonious environment that endures long after the sale of the property is consummated."

Throughout her career, Thomas' goal has included fulfilling her clients' needs as a full service agency, while promoting Savannah's positive attributes nationally and

internationally. These efforts have succeeded in positioning the firm as Savannah's marketplace real estate leader and one of the South's leading sources for fine real estate.

Recently, the firm was selected as Savannah's exclusive affiliate of the prestigious Sotheby's International Realty, the world's premier residential real estate brokerage house. Additionally, the firm was welcomed into The Estates Club, an international elite organization comprised of the world's leading real estate firms. As a member of Who's Who in Luxury Real Estate, an international compendium of luxury brokers, the agency was selected based on the criteria of "exceptional knowledge and expertise in marketing in-city mansions, states, waterfront retreats, gentlemen's farms and ranches, resort properties, and literally, the finest residences in the world."

In addition to the firm's brokerage activity, it owns and operates the largest property management rental company in Savannah, with more than 500 units representing the full spectrum of Savannah real estate. From the Landmark Historic District to the coastal islands, the residential and commercial rental firm offers a variety of lifestyle or business options to fill every need.

■ Granite Steps Inn.

Thomas has a long history of participation and leadership in the area's significant commercial developments, beginning with the creation of Savannah's City Market in 1983. It was her vision that spearheaded the development of a 100,000-square-foot marketplace featuring shopping, restaurants and entertainment. Her drive and persistence have also resulted in a phenomenal record of growth as her relationship with the Savannah College of Art and Design (SCAD) and her efforts led to the acquisition and restoration of more than 50 individual properities located in the Historic District by SCAD. More recently, she was privileged to be an active participant in the development of Savannah's resort and convention hub on Hutchinson Island.

As a top resource in marketing inner-city neighborhoods and in the preserving of historic properties, Cora Bett's expertise has been sought after by historic preservation professionals from around the country. She has become an acknowledged historic real estate expert as a guest speaker for the National Trust for Historic Preservation at its national annual conference.

Through the years, her community service has included work as a Vestry Member of Christ Episcopal Church, a member of the City's Zoning Board of Appeals where she worked with the Savannah Economic Development Association and the Historic Savannah Foundation, and as a board member of the Savannah Area Chamber of Commerce, SAFE Shelter, and The Beach Institute.

With the leadership of Cora Bett Thomas, the professionalism of her staff, and the combination of technology and old world ambiance in a centralized location, Cora Bett Thomas Realty Company is the perfect place to start when seeking a gracious introduction to the Savannah community.

■ Gaucho's on Broughton Street.

Coldwell Banker Greater Savannah Realty

We're saving time for the customer by creating convenience.

Coldwell Banker Greater Savannah Realty has become one of the most successful and recognized real estate companies in Southeast Georgia and the South Carolina Lowcountry by offering its customers a "one-stop shopping experience." By offering assistance with the search for real estate to applying for a loan and even moving in, the team at Coldwell Banker Greater Savannah Realty makes finding a home a quick, easy, and pleasurable experience.

■ Connie Farmer Ray, co-owner of Coldwell Banker Greater Savannah Realty.

Locally owned and operated by Connie Farmer Ray and Glenda Ganem, the company has grown into a market leader that prides itself in Southern hospitality and real estate professionalism. Opened in the spring of 1995, Coldwell Banker Greater Savannah Realty has grown to more than 110 sales associates and $100 million in residential and commercial sales.

Connie Farmer Ray is the energetic community leader behind the company's growth. "We are excited about our position in the market," said Ray. "With our wide range of resources, we now have the unique opportunity to provide more services to our customers." Ms. Ray attributes their explosive success to a number of reasons including a dedicated and hard working team of sales agents, managers, and staff personnel, an incredible resource of tools, education, and support offered by Coldwell Banker and the trust of all of their clients and customers over the past five years.

■ "With our wide range of resources, we now have the unique opportunity to provide more services to our customers," says Ray.

Ms. Ray comments that, "We strive to offer a 'one stop shopping experience' by offering a multitude of services including Residential and Commercial real estate sales, Property Management, Corporate Relocation Services, New Home Sales Center, Concierge Services, and even a Greater Savannah School of Real Estate."

Ms. Ray says, "Savannah is an easy sell. It is like a small metropolitan city which offers the finest, culturally, that you can have and at the same time, it can still be laid back. Savannah has a good mix. The people are diverse as well as the housing styles and communities." Ray continues, "We pride ourselves by staying on the cutting edge in the real estate industry. We continue to research and explore new ideas on increasing our services to our clients and customers. We strive to utilize the Internet to its fullest by offering virtual tours of homes and making ourselves available through websites and e-mail. We even offer a complete Concierge Department that will simplify the move-in process by offering to assist in handling utilities or repairs of a home."

"One stop shopping is the future of our company. We will continue to offer services, technology, and most importantly a personal touch on every facet of our clients and customer real estate needs," says Ms. Ray.

J.T. Turner Construction Co., Inc.

Renovation of the historic district captured Turner's interest.

When Jim Turner founded J.T. Turner Construction Co., Inc. in 1976, his primary goal was to pursue new commercial and residential construction opportunities available in the City of Savannah. However, after two short years, renovation of the historic district captured Turner's interest. The challenge of transforming neglected historic sites back to their original glory became truly appealing to the newcomer.

■ J.T. Turner, Jr.—President. Established 1976.

A native of Thomasville, Georgia, Turner later found himself in Macon, where he graduated from Mercer University in 1973. His background in banking afforded him a solid financial insight and knowledge of today's complex business world. His experience with various construction companies aided in the development of his skills as a professional. These two aspects, combined with Turner's dedication and passion for the renovation of Savannah's famous historic district, have allowed J.T. Turner Construction Co., Inc. to become the established, respected company that it is today.

J.T. Turner Construction Co., Inc. now boasts approximately 40 employees, including full-time project managers and experienced carpenters. Turner's commitment to fine craftsmanship and detail is one of the main reasons he oversees each project personally. In addition to project managers and carpenters, a well-balanced administrative staff keeps the office of J.T. Turner Construction Co., Inc. operating smoothly.

Turner's list of renovation accomplishments includes such historical landmarks as the award-winning Juliette Gordon Lowe National Birthplace, the Owens-Thomas Museum, and the Anson and Lazarus Mohr House, which was featured on the *This Old House* show in 1996. His commercial successes include the construction of the Mighty 8th Air Force Heritage Museum, the YMCA in Hinesville, Georgia, and the Skidaway Island Library. Turner has completed numerous commercial buildings and medical projects throughout the community. In addition to these projects, Turner has expanded into insurance repairs. J.T. Turner Construction Co., Inc. is listed as a preferred contractor for numerous insurance companies, and boasts a 24-hour emergency response team, ensuring immediate attention for his clients.

■ Owens–Thomas Museum—Savannah, Georgia.

The Historic Savannah Foundation and the Georgia Trust for Historical Preservation have awarded Jim Turner and his team numerous awards throughout the years for their contributions to the City of Savannah and for the integral part he has played in the revitalization of the downtown area. Turner's integrity and professionalism, combined with his business sense and devotion to the preservation of historic properties, have created a business that has made an indelible mark on the City of Savannah.

Health Care & Education

Isi Sarfati

Georgia Southern University

Georgia Southern brings the resources of one of the state's major universities to a region loaded with economic potential ready to develop.

■ Georgia Southern awards bachelors, masters, and doctoral degrees to more than 2,300 graduates a year. More than 5,000 university alumni make their homes in the Savannah area.

To the delight of parents and students of Savannah and Chatham County, one of the state's largest and most comprehensive universities is less than an hour's drive away. Situated in a lush part of southern Georgia where pleasant climates, a thriving historic port city, and nearby beaches beckon, Georgia Southern's campus is located in one of the nicest small cities in Georgia, filled with college conveniences.

The University's eye-catching range of contemporary, modern facilities blends well with its traditional architecture reflecting nearly a century of history. The 634-acre campus is a park-like panorama of lakes, lawns, spreading oaks, sweet magnolias, and soaring pines. The historic center of the campus is located on the campus green on Sweetheart Circle, surrounded by the three original buildings of red brick and columned porticos. The major academic buildings and student centers are linked throughout the campus by the double-lane Pedestrium, a walking mall tiled with earthtone pavers. Fountains, plazas, and benches offer niches for respite and reflection along the lamp-lined walkways, creating environment for learning and living Georgia Southern students love and remember.

As the largest and most comprehensive center of higher education in the southern half of Georgia, the institution is third in student enrollment among the state universities. A residential campus of 14,400 students, Georgia Southern is one of the top two universities of choice in Georgia for new freshman, including HOPE Scholars; every state and 80 nations are represented in the student body. Today, nearly 900 Georgia Southern students and 3,500 alumni are Chatham County residents.

The friendly campus is filled with plusses. In its decade as a University, Georgia Southern has invested more than $122 million in a renaissance of buildings and beautification. The learning environment for students and the public is enhanced by a museum of cultural and natural history, a botanical garden, and a unique wildlife education center.

■ Georgia Southern ranks as the state's third largest university campus and reaches across the Coastal Empire and South Georgia through centers in Savannah, Brunswick, Hinesville, Dublin, and Augusta.

Those assests grow out of an intriguing history that has taken the school from a small college to a sprawling university. The campus was founded in 1906 as one of 11 agricultural and mechanical schools chartered by the legislature to give each congressional district an educational center specializing in modern farming and technology. Statesboro and Bulloch County, about 45 miles from Savannah, outbid its neighboring communities for the location of the school with an offer of $125,000 in start-up cash and 300 acres on the outskirts of town. Most of the district A&M schools lived on to become college campuses, but Georgia Southern has been by far the most successful, earning university status in 1990 as Georgia's first university in the southern half of the state.

As a school situated in a mostly rural part of Georgia, Georgia Southern University has attracted quite a national following. With sporting events frequently televised, the Georgia Southern Eagles are constantly in the spotlight, competing nationally in intercollegiate sports on the Division I level, with winning records that have earned nationally-televised season appearances in football, basketball, baseball, and golf. The Eagles made history by winning five NCAA I-AA National Football Championships—1985, 1986, 1989, 1990, and 1999—a record unequalled in the division.

Academically, the university excels in every category. Georgia Southern's hallmark is a superior undergraduate experience emphasizing academic distinction, excellent teaching, and student success. Teaching is first priority; professors teach every course, while personal attention is the key to student achievement. Through more selective admission standards, Georgia Southern is enhancing its academic profile. An expanded scholarship Honors Program, and targeted recruiting of academically-talented students is expected to attract even more outstanding students from further reaches of the country.

Accredited by the Southern Association of Colleges and Schools, Georgia Southern offers more than 130 undergraduate and graduate degree programs through the doctoral level in six colleges: Liberal Arts and Social Sciences, Business Administration; Education; Health and

Professional Studies; The Jack N. Averitt College of Graduate Studies; and the Allen E. Paulson College of Science and Technology. The university has earned national accreditation in 20 program areas. Outside the major research universities in Athens and Atlanta, Georgia Southern offers more academic degree programs with more national accreditations than any university in the state.

Georgia Southern serves its mostly rural coastal region through outreach and research in economic development, education, cultural opportunities, rural health, and environmental interests. The university extends educational opportunities throughout the region at graduate centers in Savannah, Augusta, Brunswick, Hinesville, Dublin, and at numerous remote sites statewide via distance learning.

One of the university's most interesting aspects is its diverse range of specialized departments and unique museums and exhibits.

The university's Center for Wildlife Education and Lamar Q. Ball Raptor Center is a 15-acre oasis of eco-diversity populated by bald eagles, hawks, and other birds of prey in mini-habitats very like their natural homes. The Center's nature walks allow its thousands of visitors to get up-close-and-personal with native wildlife in open air habitats. Falconers put on a daily high-speed air show of hawks and other hunting birds, while down-to-earth live exhibits of local reptiles and mammals populate the ecology education building.

■ The Georgia Southern Eagles earned the "Team of the Century" title in NCAA I-AA football when they won an unprecedented total of five national championships: 1985, 1986, 1989, 1990, and 1999.

Meanwhile, just minutes away from a show of wildlife, the toothy grin of a 25-foot fossil skeleton of a mosasaur—"the T-Rex of the sea"—greets visitors at the popular University Museum. The nationally-accredited museum showcases the cultural and natural history of the southern coast from prehistoric eras to the present, and hosts traveling exhibits from museums around the nation.

Located adjacent to the campus, an 11-acre Botanical Garden lies on what was once the farm of a local botanist, where the original homestead cottage, forest, and fields are now an ecological center for native plants and animals of the southeastern coastal plain. The attractions don't stop there. The largest tick collection in the world—more than a million specimens—belongs to the Smithsonian Institution but resides at Georgia Southern's world-class research institute on disease-carrying parasites. The collection is a natural treasure and a world-wide source for identification of ticks and related research on the diseases they carry.

Georgia Southern students and faculty are never lost for entertainment options. In 2001, the university will open its expanded continuing education and conference center and 850-seat theater for the performing arts, the largest in the region outside Savannah. This will raise the curtain for world-class performances which students and South Georgia citizens could never see without traveling to a major metropolitan area.

Georgia Southern brings the resources of one of the state's major universities to a region loaded with economic potential ready to develop. In partnership with business, government, and education, the university is working to build an enterprise environment through initiatives in business research, engineering and information technology, professional graduate programs, international trade, community development, rural health, education, and tourism. A major role for the university is increasing the value of the region's intellectual capital, both human resources and knowledge base. More than a dozen university centers serve regional interests—for example the logistics and intermodal transportation program, which has strong ties with the Georgia Ports Authority located in Savannah.

■ The Wildlife Education Center's bald eagles are the main attraction for thousands of visitors who can get up close and personal with native wildlife in open air habitats.

To better serve prospective students in and around the university, Georgia Southern manages the University System's Coastal Georgia Center, which centralizes off-campus graduate programs offered by local universities and is a growing venue to promote economic development and public service. The Center offers a technologically-advanced learning environment for professional development and other corporate educational needs. And in addition to the Coastal Center, the university has also expanded graduate programs to the region through centers in Brunswick, Hinesville, Augusta,and Dublin.

As Georgia Southern University continues to attract students, faculty, and an expanding list of new programs, its campus remains to be a multi-faceted benefit to the citizens of south Georgia.

Savannah College of Art and Design

The college brings culture, vitality, and a tremendous economic boost to the Savannah community.

■ THE FOUNDERS' UNIQUE METHOD OF CREATING A COLLEGE CAMPUS BY RECYCLING OLD BUILDINGS—SUCH AS POETTER HALL—HAS BROUGHT ACCLAIM TO THE CITY AND TO THE COLLEGE AS WELL.

From West Boundary Street to East Broad, from the riverfront to the southern end of Martin Luther King Jr. Boulevard, the Savannah College of Art and Design has taken a leading role in restoring and preserving Savannah's architectural treasures. The creative energy of students, faculty, and staff has breathed new life into Savannah's renowned National Historic Landmark District, generating hundreds of millions of dollars for the local economy.

The founders' unique method of creating a college campus by recycling old buildings has brought acclaim to the city and to the college as well. The Savannah College of Art and Design has been recognized by the Historic Savannah Foundation, the Georgia Trust for Historic Preservation, the Art Deco Societies of America, the American Institute of Architects, the National Trust for Historic Preservation, and the International Downtown Association.

■ THE STUDENT BODY NUMBERS APPROXIMATELY 5,000, WITH STUDENTS COMING FROM ALL 50 STATES AND MORE THAN 80 COUNTRIES. THE STAFF AND FACULTY NUMBER ABOUT 1,000.

A Unique Campus

The college's flagship building, Poetter Hall, is situated in the heart of the historic district. Originally the Savannah Volunteer Guards Armory, today it houses classrooms and offices for the graphic design and admission departments.

From this hub, the college has spread throughout the historic district and into the Victorian district, finding new uses for significant buildings that had outlived their 18th- and 19th-century purposes. Along Martin Luther King Jr. Boulevard, an abandoned bank has become an art gallery, a vacant warehouse is now a book and supply store, the former Central of Georgia Railroad complex serves as classrooms and studios for the college's School of Building Arts and the International Studies Center, and a former dry goods store now houses photography studios, darkrooms, and digital imaging labs. Broughton Street revitalization has been enhanced with the college's renovation of a former department store to become an 85,000-square-foot art and design library. A 1940s theater is the college's performing arts center, and a turn-of-the-century home for widows houses computer animation and interactive media classrooms.

The interweaving of the college campus within residential and business districts has updated General James Oglethorpe's original city plan of wards or neighborhoods centered around common green spaces. The city's lush squares serve as outdoor living rooms for residents, meeting spaces for business people, and inspiration for artists. To accommodate the housing needs of an increasing student population, the college acquired former motels, turning them into residence halls, complete with dining facilities and computer homework labs.

Skilled and Talented Professionals

The educated professional work force provided by graduates and the skilled part-time work force provided by students make Savannah a desirable place for doing business. The college was founded in 1978 with the mission of preparing talented students for careers in the visual and performing arts, design, building arts, and the history of art and architecture. This mission has served the college and the city of Savannah well.

Not only has the college recycled buildings and breathed new life into them, but the infusion of thousands of creative, enthusiastic, and talented artists into the city has contributed to a renewed cultural atmosphere in Savannah. The college hosts world-renowned artists, authors, lecturers, and performers each year, providing an eclectic calendar of events open to the public. Recent guests have included Tony Bennett, Helen Frankenthaler, Amy Tan, Christo and Jeanne-Claude, Betye Saar, and Maya Angelou.

The Savannah College of Art and Design is a private, nonprofit, accredited institution awarding bachelor of architecture, bachelor of fine arts, master of architecture, master of arts, and master of fine arts degrees. The college offers 18 majors: architectural history, architecture, art history, computer art, fashion, fibers, furniture design, graphic design, historic preservation, illustration, interior design, media and performing arts, metals and jewelry, painting, photography, product design, sequential art, and video/film. Minors are offered in each of the major programs as well as in decorative arts, drawing, electronic design, museum studies, printmaking, sculpture, sound design, and writing.

Diversity

The student body numbers approximately 5,000, with students coming from all 50 states and more than 80 countries. The staff and faculty number about 1,000. Class size is small, allowing each student the opportunity to receive individual attention. Professors in every major hold terminal degrees in their areas of expertise or are otherwise outstanding in their fields.

A strong English as a Second Language program and dedicated international center staff assist international students with the adjustment to college life in the United States.

The college operates several on-campus galleries featuring rotating displays in a variety of media by nationally and internationally acclaimed artists, in addition to work by students, faculty, and alumni. Recently, the college has exhibited works by Jacob Lawrence, Helen Frankenthaler, Andy Warhol, Jasper Johns, Romare Bearden, Miriam Schapiro, Audrey Flack, and Christo and Jeanne-Claude.

■ Not only has the college recycled buildings and breathed new life into them, but the infusion of thousands of creative, enthusiastic, and talented artists into the city has contributed to a renewed cultural atmosphere in Savannah.

■ The Savannah College of Art and Design operates several on-campus galleries that exhibit rotating displays of work by students, faculty, and nationally and internationally acclaimed artists. Robert Rauschenberg, Laurie Simmons, Jasper Johns, Jacob Lawrence, Betye Saar, Jim Dine, Andy Warhol, and Christo and Jeanne-Claude are among the artists recently featured.

Community Events

The college sponsors a full calendar of lectures, workshops, seminars, performances, book signings, and festivals open to the public. Recent notable speakers have included Dr. Henry Louis Gates Jr., Wilma Mankiller, Amy Tan, B. D. Wong, Maurice Sendak, Danny Glover, Dith Pran, and Hal Rubenstein. Special events include the annual Sidewalk Arts Festival held the last Saturday in April in Forsyth Park. Sponsored by Coca-Cola, this popular festival features a chalk drawing contest, music, live performances, food, and a fund-raising raffle.

In addition to the massive restoration of nearly 40 historic structures, the college's contributions to the community include a citywide mural project and a variety of creative in-kind services. The college's community service coordinator matches students with volunteer opportunities, providing a useful service to both the public and private sectors.

The Savannah College of Art and Design competes at the NCAA Division III level in soccer, tennis, cross country, basketball, baseball, equestrian, softball, volleyball, rowing, and golf. The college publishes a weekly newspaper and an alumni magazine. "SCAD TV," a weekly television program produced by the college, is broadcast locally.

The meteoric growth of the college from 71 students when classes began in 1979 to about 5,000 students today has brought culture, vitality, and a tremendous economic boost to the Savannah community. Many graduates have chosen to remain in the area to work in the visual arts or design fields or to start their own businesses.

For more information about the college, programs of study or cultural events the college sponsors visit the college on the World Wide Web at www.scad.edu.

Memorial Health

A 24-hour toll-free call center means that healthcare advice is only minutes away for residents in the 35-county service area.

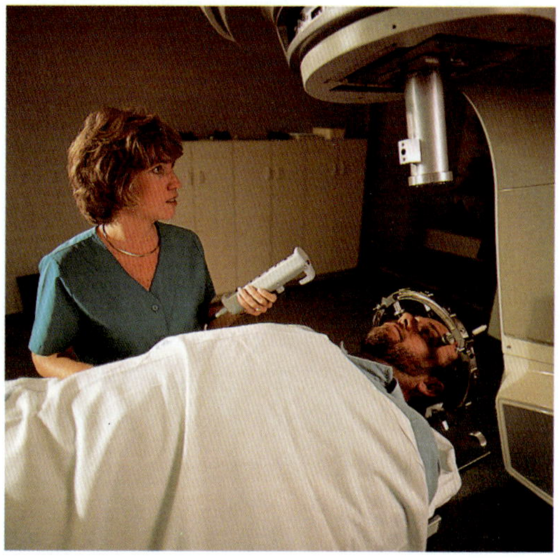

What was once a small community hospital has been transformed into a sprawling medical campus that today serves a 35-county area in southeast Georgia and southern South Carolina. Memorial Health has integrated the area's most acclaimed specialists, creating Memorial Health University Medical Center; CareOne; a network of primary and specialty care physicians; and business and industry services, completing one of the most comprehensive medical systems in the southeast.

■ THE CENTER FOR CANCER CARE OFFERS TECHNOLOGY COMPARABLE TO MAJOR CANCER CENTERS ACROSS THE COUNTRY.

Standing alone in its high-tech surroundings based in the heart of Savannah, the facility and its team of professionals have taken strides in growth to include several areas of medical services. Memorial Health University Medical Center, a 530-licensed bed tertiary medical center, has become a regional referral center for heart care,cancer care, trauma, pediatrics, high-risk obstetrics, neonatology, and rehabilitation. Services include:

The Heart and Vascular Institute, a major provider of cardiac care, offering a full range of heart programs and services from prevention through surgery, rehabilitation, and home care. As a pioneer for open heart surgery in this region, the institute offers some of the area's most comprehensive heart care treatments and facilities. After heart surgery, cardiac rehabilitation programs and the Health Institute provide the patient with follow-up care at home that includes exercise, diet management, and behavior modification.

As host of the region's most comprehensive children's hospital caring for infants and adolescents, Memorial Health combines the element of education with patient services. Pediatricians and specialists of the future train in a 41-bed unit, supported by a faculty of experts in the fields of adolescent medicine, gastroenterology, hematology, infectious disease, oncology, neurology, surgery, rehabilitation, ophthalmology, and otolaryngology. Memorial Health's Neonatal Intensive Care Nursery is one of only six Level 3 care facilities in the state of Georgia, representing the highest level of care available for premature and critically ill newborns. When transportation is necessary for these tiny babies, a specially trained team and Angel 3, a neonatal transport unit, bring newborns to Memorial's high-tech facility.

■ MEMORIAL HEALTH PIONEERED OPEN HEART SURGERY IN SAVANNAH.

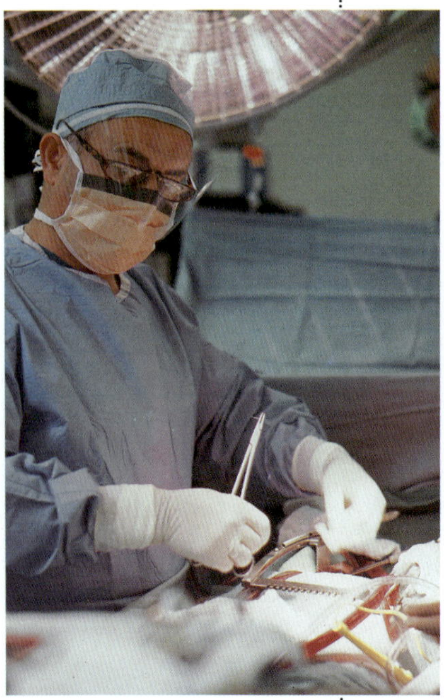

Memorial Health's outreach assistance programs reach far beyond cardiac and children's care. The healthcare professionals of the highly acclaimed Memorial Health sports medicine program bring their services to the arenas and sporting events of high school, college, and professional athletic events. A comprehensive Rehabilitation Center helps injured athletes and recovering patients regain strength and master everyday skills.

The Center for Cancer Care offers patients a team of experts, including surgeons, radiation oncologists, and medical oncologists. Technology at the center is comparable to major cancer centers across the country.

As a major teaching hospital affiliated with Mercer University School of Medicine, Memorial Health University Medical Center instructs both upcoming and experienced physicians through its six residency programs and graduate/ continuing medical education programs. With 29 physician practices in the region, Memorial Health physicians provide primary care and specialty services in smaller cities and towns. A 24-hour toll-free call center means that healthcare advice is only minutes away for residents in the 35-county service area.

Thanks to its commitment to serving southeast Georgians and South Carolinians with world-class health care, the future continues to look promising as Memorial Health follows the vision to become the healthcare provider of choice in every community it serves.

Savannah Technical College

The college's philosophy could be summarized in two words—creating opportunities.

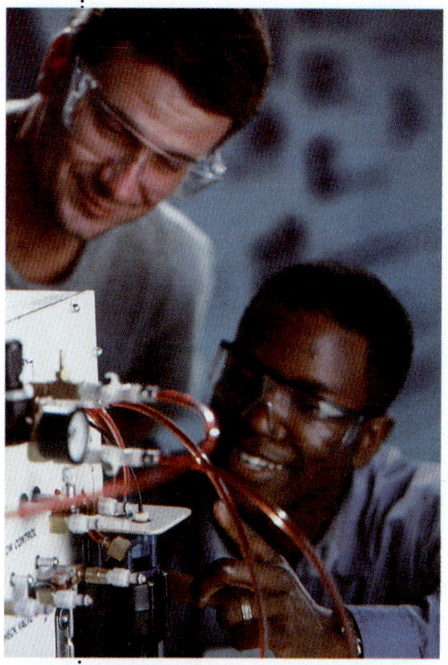

It was spring of 2000 when the nation's largest dollar-discount variety company followed other industry giants who have broken ground for new facilities in the Savannah area. The Dollar Tree proudly announced plans for a 600,000 square-foot-distribution facility creating more than 100 full-time and 80 seasonal jobs. Others, including JCBamford, The Home Depot, the Lummus Corporation, and Willamette Industries recently joined a long line of companies who have already chosen the Savannah area to locate. It's a fact. The region's economy is flourishing and with that economic boon comes a demand for employees. That's where Savannah Tech steps in to meet the demand for trained and skilled labor.

Located in the heart of Savannah and in three neighboring counties, the modern campus and branch locations house a myriad of career opportunities. From certificate programs ranging in aircraft structural assembly to carpentry framing and pharmaceutical assistants, to two-year programs in accounting and surgical technology, the college's philosophy could be summarized in two words—creating opportunities. Serving the employees and communities of Bryan, Chatham, Effingham, and Liberty counties, Savannah Technical College graduates become skilled employees who contribute to the overall economic development of the area. In short, Savannah Technical College helps sell Savannah, as well as serve its current employers.

THE SCHOOL'S CURRICULUM IS DICTATED BY LOCAL INDUSTRY NEED AND DEMAND AND THAT MEANS GRADUATES POSSESS SKILLS AND TRAINING THAT THEY CAN PUT TO USE IMMEDIATELY.

Projections indicate that 75 percent of the jobs in the future will require post-secondary training, but not a four-year degree. That's why, in Savannah, the motivation to pursue a degree requiring technical skills starts early. Ninth grade high school students are given the opportunity to pursue a "Tech Prep Seal" and a program of study to enter the job market with training in a career path that offers competitive earnings.

Programs offered at Savannah Technical College are always up-to-date. That's because the school's curriculum is dictated by local industry need and demand and that means graduates possess skills and training that they can put to use immediately. Short-term Workforce Certification Programs like the Certified Customer Service Specialist and Certified Manufacturing Specialist provide employers with applicants that possess strong foundation skills as well as the opportunity to recalibrate existing workers. Participants in the New Connections to Work and Georgia Fatherhood Program receive career counseling and assessments, life management skills workshops, technical training, job readiness workshops, and support group meetings.

WITH SAVANNAH TECH'S CONVENIENCE, AFFORDABLE COST, AND PROGRAM CURRICULUM RELEVANT TO TODAY'S WORK ENVIRONMENT, AREA STUDENTS ARE LEARNING THAT THEY'RE ONLY A FEW STEPS AWAY FROM BECOMING HIGH SKILLED AND HIGHLY PAID.

Savannah Tech is affordable! Georgia residents use the HOPE Grant and the HOPE Scholarship to cover the cost of tuition and books and other financial aid options are available to eligible students. They include the Pell Grant and veterans' benefits. Since 1995, Savannah Tech has added 25 new Quick Start projects in a four county service delivery area. This program has served Georgia as an economic development incentive for the location of new companies and as a factor in maintaining a positive business climate to encourage further business and industry expansion and investment in the state.

Savannah Tech is a unit of the Georgia Department of Technical and Adult Education, providing programs that utilize the best available technology and offer easy access to lifelong education and training for all adult Georgians and corporate citizens.

With Savannah Tech's convenience, affordable cost, and program curriculum relevant to today's work environment, area students are learning that they're only a few steps away from becoming high skilled and highly paid.

The Marketplace

Li-Wen Lee

ANNAH'S CANDY KITCHEN

Chatham County

Chatham County continues to climb in the rankings as one of the southeast's fastest-growing areas for industry, recreation, and tourism.

From the picturesque seas of the Atlantic Ocean and its beautiful Tybee Island beaches to the pine forests of its western suburbs, Chatham County is a land rich in beauty, natural resources, and industrious leadership. With its courthouse standing tall in the midst of the downtown area and local government officials headquartered in an historic building on Wright Square, Chatham County continues to climb in the rankings as one of the southeast's fastest-growing areas for industry, recreation, and tourism.

The Administrative/Legislative Court House houses the County Manager's office and other department heads and is where the Chatham County Commission meets. Photo by Peter Nichols.

Touting the country's largest historic district of 2.5 square miles, Chatham County continues to be the ideal setting for corporate meetings, vacationers, and retreats. Boasting Old World charm while remaining an easily traveled area, residents and visitors can choose their mode of transportation, whether it's by foot, bike, or car.

Savannah's 45 cultural attractions have long been a draw, but Savannah's natural environment is fast becoming one of its most popular fascinations. The development of eco- or nature-based tourism offers true-life adventures as the Atlantic Ocean and Intracoastal waterways, along with miles and miles of marshlands that provide captive audiences with first-hand views of wildlife in action.

All across the 25-mile County area are signs of prosperity. On one of this county's newest assets—neighboring Hutchinson Island—an $83 million trade center beckons conventioneers from all across the world. Beside the trade center stands a gleaming new, 400-room hotel and just across the water on the Savannah side and more than 9,000 hotel and motel rooms await tourists eager to sample the area.

Home to the Judicial Branch of Chatham County Government. Photo by Peter Nichols.

■ To promote healthy gardens and low water use during drought conditions, the Chatham County Cooperative Extension Center planted and maintains a "xeriscape garden." Photo by Peter Nichols.

With accommodations so prevalent and a modern trade center to accommodate even more visitors, predictions are that business travel to the area will increase by 20 percent. Promoting those figures is the ability of the area to attract visitors from all over the country. Today, Savannah is linked to several other major cities, as direct flights are currently available from the Savannah International Airport to Miami, Cincinnati, Washington, D.C., Chicago, Houston, and Atlanta.

Boasting an excellent education system that includes two major universities, a world-renowned art college, and several smaller colleges, Chatham County's educational resources abound. Private schools are plentiful and Savannah's rich traditions of history and flourishing eco-system provide the perfect breeding ground for learning. Filled with residential communities, varying from traditional homes to contemporary townhomes and condominiums overlooking scenic waterways, the county's housing options offer homes and neighborhoods for varying income levels and tastes. A unique environment with mild temperatures year-round offers the perfect atmosphere for a variety of outdoor activities.

The Chatham County Department of Parks and Recreation supports several outdoor facilities including boat ramps and piers, parks, and an outstanding aquatic center. With a state-of-the-art facade, a bubble dome marks the spot of this amazing complex. Complete with a snack bar, a pro shop, nautilus weight equipment, bleachers, and ample parking, the center plays host to major swimming championships hosted year-round. Additionally, a municipal golf course, a world-class track and field complex (that seats 6,300), and the Anderson Cohen Weightlifting Center are home to Olympic athletes in training and locals inspired to train on their own. Thanks to the efforts of the Chatham County leadership, the area alone boasts more than 200 parks and recreational facilities, and public facilities include seven fishing piers, nine public boat ramps, nine tennis courts, four stables, and five public golf courses.

■ County Commission Chairman Dr. Billy Hair and Vice Chairman Dr. Priscilla Thomas congratulate the graduating seniors of the Chatham County Youth Commission. Youth Commission members are selected from every high school in Chatham County and during their term, members of the Youth Commission sit in and take part in County Commission meetings. This Youth Commission has become a model for other Youth Commissions throughout the country. Photo by Peter Nichols.

Chatham County is a haven for new industry. In 1999, the area was the state's second fastest-growing metropolitan area (for employment). Projections are that it will take the lead in the future. Industrial giants like Dollar Tree Stores, Inc., The Home Depot, The Lummas Corporation, and JCBanford make their presence in Chatham County along a hearty stretch of Interstate 95, near the railroad and the bustling, world-class, Georgia Ports Authority. Within the county's location is an ideal setting for industry that is strengthened by collaborative approaches for development among the local Chamber of Commerce, the City of Savannah, Chatham County government, and the Savannah Economic Development Authority.

Statewide tax incentives have also played a role in attracting new industry to Chatham County. The Georgia Department of Labor's hiring assistance program, Quick Start training programs, the unique assistance program offered by Georgia Technical Institute and the Hope Scholarship Program are valuable incentives that have strengthened Chatham County's economic health.

The lighthouse at Tybee Island glows with Comet Hale-Bopp behind it. Photo by Perry Sapp.

Chatham County's new International Maritime Trade and Convention Center. Photo compliments of Savannah/Chatham Trade Center Authority.

A scenic view of the many salt marshes in Chatham County. Photo by Peter Nichols.

Selected in 1999 as one of the *New York Times'* top 12 trendy worldwide hot spots, and as one of *Conde Nast* Traveler's Top 10 Places to Live in the Country in 2000, at least 17 corporations make the Chatham County their headquarters. Those companies include Gulfstream Aerospace Corporation where more than 1,000 aircraft have been produced for corporate, government, private, and military customers worldwide and the Lummus Corporation, manufacturer of cotton ginning and other textile machinery.

Also drawn to the area were 14 Fortune 500 Companies located in and around Savannah, as well as 28 international firms, including names like Bell Equipment N.A., Inc. and E.M. Industries, a division of EM Industries' Chemicals and Pigments Division.

Indeed, Chatham County geography, lifestyle, and tradition make it the perfect oasis for vacationing or living. With Old World charm, high-tech abilities, and strong local leadership, it remains to be one of this country's most valued treasures.

A recent Chatham County Commission Meeting had a special opening as the Colors were presented by the Marine Color Guard from Parris Island, South Carolina. Photo by Peter Nichols.

The City of Savannah

Oglethorpe unveiled a plan for an orderly town that would consist of 24 squares placed at regular intervals.

From the 23-karat gold dome that crowns City Hall to the impressive cable-span bridge that links Savannah to South Carolina's shores, signs of thoughtful planning are evident throughout this picturesque city. Savannah's past has been delicately preserved and, along with careful planning, this city has become one of the country's most popular places to visit and live. Indeed, Savannah's leaders have fine-tuned the art of balancing the city's delicate historical fabric with the needs of the future. But long before her popularity began making national headlines, a lush shoreline with its steep bluff overlooking the river caught the eye of a curious explorer and visionary. Seeking a place as an asylum for debtors, in 1733, British General James Oglethorpe staked his claim on a high bluff, naming it Savannah, and chartered Georgia, the 13th colony in the name of King George II. With sights set on functionality, Oglethorpe unveiled a plan for an orderly town that would consist of 24 squares placed at regular intervals. Today, his plan is still heralded as a mark of outstanding engineering by students and city planners all over the world and Savannah claims the title of being "America's first planned city."

Through the years, the city has maintained Oglethorpe's plan, preserving it through meticulous and constant care and judicious planning. Today, Savannah's 22 remaining squares, and dozens of parks and public spaces throughout the City, provide lush settings for the numerous festivals, concerts, and cultural events which are held year-round, and provided by the City to residents and guests, free of charge. Those same parks and squares offer residents the perfect settings for nice, afternoon strolls.

Not only known as "America's first planned city," Savannah is also referred to as "The Hostess City of the South," a nickname well deserved due to the City's hospitable reputation. The live oaks draped in Spanish Moss, the vast fields of azaleas, the fountains and monuments, and other public art... none are accidents, but the result of careful planning and daily, year-round maintenance by City workers who care, and who are guided by a City Council with vision and foresight. Savannah encompasses a 2.5 mile Historic District—the largest urban historic district in the country, and, serves as one of the country's most popular vacation spots. But unlike other communities, Savannah's Historic District is not a museum piece...it's a living, breathing neighborhood, where residents live, shop, and dine along with the millions of guests who visit each year.

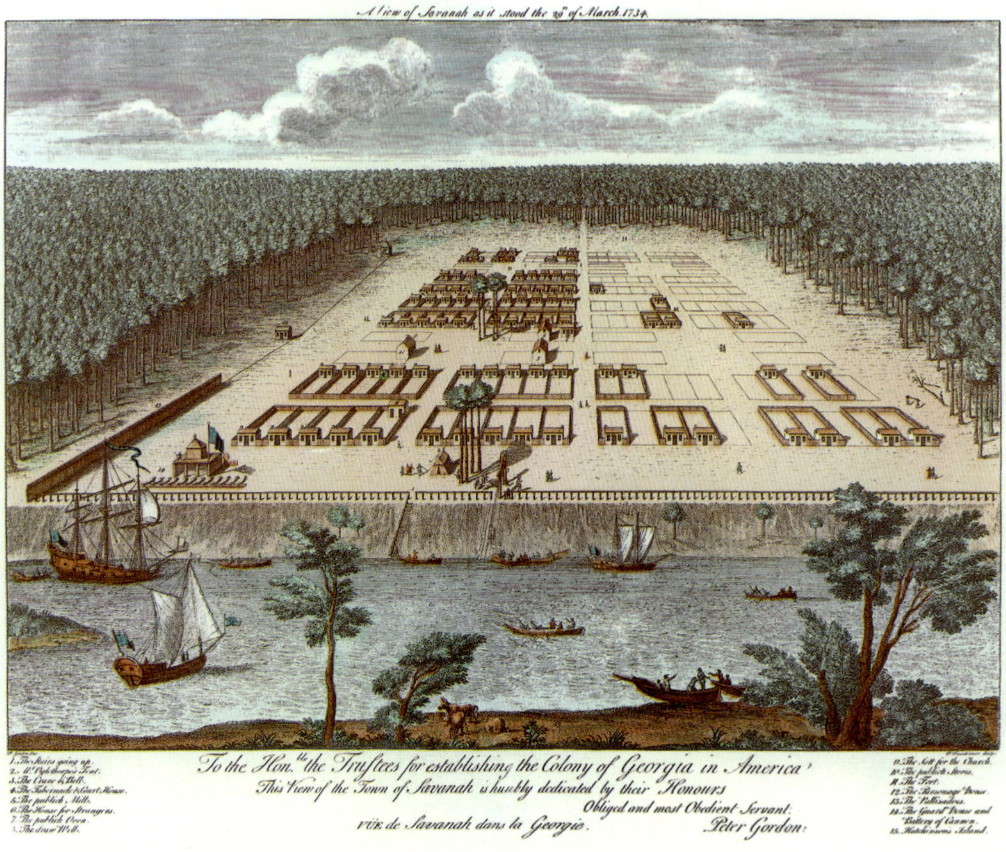

Savannah's Historic District makes up just one part of a very progressive and diverse community. Growth in industry and an expanding job market have made Savannah one of the fastest growing cities in the state. The City has many programs aimed at fostering economic development and growth, including small and minority-owned business assistance, low interest loans, job training assistance, etc. In addition, the Savannah Economic Development Authority (SEDA) is one organization partly responsible for bringing new jobs to the city and it has earned one of the most prestigious reputations in the country for doing just that. With the islands and beaches to the east, growth to the west and south has been phenomenal, and, as a result, there is no lack of shopping, dining, or recreational opportunities.

The view of Savannah's Riverfront has changed considerably since Oglethorpe landed, but the emphasis on historical preservation is apparent. City Hall can be seen from the Trade Center and Resort, just three minutes by ferry across the Savannah River.

New facilities combine with the old to create a market for tourists that runs year-round as opposed to seasonal, bringing about an abundance of economic prosperity. An $83 million Savannah International Maritime Trade and Convention Center, replete with highly advanced multi-media technology, is just one sign that history and tourism can grow a city without posing a threat. A three-minute ride across the Savannah River by water ferry provides an impressive link to a $98 million hotel that boasts nearly 400-rooms and a Greenbrier spa. And on Savannah's own shores lie more than 9,000 hotel and motel rooms.

The City's Film Commission Office has helped facilitate Savannah's rise in popularity. Dozens of full-length movies have been made here, including "Forrest Gump," "The Garden of Good and Evil," "The Legend of Bagger Vance," and many, many more. These and other productions filmed in the city have had the effect of showcasing Savannah's assets to literally millions of film fans. The film industry alone has graced the economy with a whopping $20 million in a single year!

Today, Oglethorpe's bluff is filled with colorful pubs, shops, and restaurants. Across the waterfront, an enormous trade center casts an impressive reflection in the busy Savannah River, reminding Savannahians of all cultures that careful planning, combined with progressive leadership, lead to a city filled with prosperity.

As tourists look on, millions of tons of cargo pass right through Savannah's Historic District, on the way to the Savannah Port, one of the busiest and most modern ports in the Southeast.

The Hilton Savannah DeSoto

Today, The Hilton Savannah DeSoto continues its reign as Savannah's grand hotel.

After a long day of business or travel, the evening begins with happy hour specials and continues with dinner at the elegant dining facilities in the Hilton Savannah DeSoto.

Amid the splendor of moss-draped live oaks, architectural masterpieces, and ornate fountains towers Savannah's grand hotel, The Hilton Savannah DeSoto, a true Southern landmark. This site has spawned an impressive historical narrative and today, a newly refurbished hotel still crowns the Savannah skyline with first-class accommodations, upscale cuisine, and jazzy nightlife.

A festive New Year's Day society ball christened the hotel in 1890 and set the stage for years of energy and opulence. Characterized by its Romanesque architecture, more than five United States presidents have graced the halls of The DeSoto. Celebrities from Lady Astor, Margaret Mitchell, Lillian Russell, Gregory Peck and Katherine Hepburn have sampled the hotel's luxurious rooms and suites in years past.

The Hilton Savannah DeSoto is surrounded by magnificently restored homes, historic churches, and moss-draped oaks in the heart of Savannah's Historic District.

Today, The Hilton Savannah DeSoto continues its reign as Savannah's grand hotel. Purchased in 1996 by MHI Hotels—a privately held corporation specializing in hotel management and operations—the company's reputation for renovating, restoring and successfully operating older hotel properties is evident in the quality of service displayed at this Savannah showplace. The recently renovated DeSoto is still engulfed in history, but is set in fine furnishings, antiques, and reproductions, all freshly displayed.

Located in the heart of the Historic District in downtown Savannah, the hotel is within walking distance of charming boutiques, quaint coffee shops and fine restaurants, all set amid the city's 21 original squares. The adventuresome may hop aboard a

HARBORVIEW ROOM LOCATED ATOP THE HILTON ON THE 15TH FLOOR. AVAILABLE FOR GROUPS UP TO 125.

carriage for a leisurely trip through the Historic District. If golf is the game of choice, choose from one of the many area courses located within 15 minutes of the hotel. When the stars beckon, there's a lobby-side bar, The Lion's Den, that features daily drink specials and live music on the weekends.

The hotel's 12th floor was recently converted to a Hilton Honors floor. Comprised of all king rooms with full, extra-long beds, it complements the 13th floor concierge level. In addition, authentic Lowcountry cuisine is offered in the hotel's popular Magnolia Restaurant. An outdoor heated pool offers a refreshing respite from the city below and the view of Savannah's skyline from that deck is unprecedented.

For a city made famous by history, The Hilton Savannah DeSoto continues to make its own history with convention services that include 20,000 square feet of flexible meeting space, along with a full convention service department.

The Savannah experience is not complete without a stay in the city's premier hotel showcase, The Hilton Savannah DeSoto.

GUESTS CAN TAKE ADVANTAGE OF A PANORAMIC VIEW IN THE ROOFTOP SWIMMING POOL.

Byrd Cookie Company

Byrd Cookie Company's clients today include Sea World, Disney, and Neiman Marcus, to name only a few.

Savannah's beauty may lie in enchanting architecture and bountiful gardens, but few realize that the city made famous by its southern elegance also boasts another nationally known treasure...Byrd Cookie Company. For more than 76 years, one family has created morsels so tasty that their fame has spread from a humble backyard shanty to theme parks and gourmet gift shops all over the country.

As one of the city's oldest family-owned businesses and an honored recipient of the Georgia Family Business of the Year award, Byrd Cookie Company has enjoyed phenomenal growth in the last decade. A major player in the gourmet cookie market, Byrd Cookie Company's clients today include Sea World, Disney, and Neiman Marcus, to name only a few. With mail order sales skyrocketing and a new 65,000-square-foot plant in full operation, the company has earned its reputation as a specialty food leader committed to providing only the highest quality products and outstanding customer service.

In 1990, Byrd's remarkably popular Key Lime Cooler Cookies were the very first cookies ever to win the "Outstanding Dessert Award" in international competition at the National Association of the Specialty Food Trade's Fancy Food Show.

But even though these tiny treats have brought Byrd Cookie Company much acclaim, the family has never lost sight of the importance of personal commitment. Today, there are five family members, comprising the third and fourth generations of the family, guiding the company. In 1997, Byrd bought out its largest competitor, the Atlanta-based Seckinger-Lee Company. The acquisition both expanded their market and significantly increased the range of gourmet products offered.

■ As consumers continue to enjoy the tiny, delectable cookies created by a legacy, they all agree on one thing. Byrd Cookies are becoming more than just a satisfying treat. They're becoming a passion.

How It All Got Started

The Byrd Cookie Company success story begins like a nostalgic novel. In 1924 Ben T. Byrd, Sr. began making cookies by hand, packing them in wooden boxes and delivering them in a Model-T Ford to Savannah stores. Word quickly spread around town that Byrd's cookies were simply the best. When Savannahians began serving Byrd cookies at afternoon tea, formal dinner parties, and during the five o'clock cocktail hour, people far and wide became loyal customers.

As the demand for Byrd's cookies increased, production also expanded. During those early years, a family-made assembly line allowed the company to bake nine dozen cookies every seven minutes. In 1927, just three years after he started his business, Mr. Byrd moved the bakery to Norwood Avenue.

Shortly after World War II, B.T. Byrd, Jr. began to manage the thriving business. He created a new line of small gourmet cookies and cocktail snacks using the benne seed as the "secret ingredient." A delicate cookie, the Benne Wafer, is still a local favorite. As the business continued to prosper, a new and larger plant was built in 1950 on four acres of land directly across the street. A retail store was added next to this bakery in 1957, and the store was christened "the Cookie Shanty."

Savannah's Byrd Cookie fans were joined by cookie lovers from all parts of the country as tour buses began making the Cookie Shanty a regular stop on their daily tours. The family was bombarded with calls and letters from customers hoping the delicious cookies could be mailed to them or to their friends as gifts. Soon Byrd Cookie Company added a mail-order division to meet this demand.

Throughout the years, Ben T. Byrd, Jr. made many changes to his facility, but he always remained on the Norwood site. Whenever more space was needed, it was simply tacked onto the existing building, forming a hodge-podge of space that eventually grew to 15,000 square feet.

For more than 76 years, one family has created morsels so tasty that their fame has spread from a humble backyard shanty to theme parks and gourmet gift shops all over the country. Pictured left to right: Cynthia Curl Harn, Stephanie Curl Lindley, Benny Curl, Shawn Curl, and Kay Byrd Curl.

When Mr. Byrd, Jr. retired in 1988, Benny Curl, son-in-law to B.T., Jr., and his wife, Kay Byrd Curl, along with their daughter, Stephanie Curl Lindley, bought the business. They immediately took responsibility for existing operations and continued development of the 64-year-old company. It was only a matter of time until the hometown bakery began making national headlines.

The Cookie Empire

With the Curl family at the helm, this business that started in the '20s soon soared into the '90s with a bright, new look. Introducing a new company logo, new designs, and artwork for the tins, and innovative cookie flavors such as Key Lime Coolers, Razzberry Tarts, and Peach Zingers, the company experienced more than a 500 percent increase in sales during the first seven years. New, smaller packaging also attracted the attention of large corporations; and in 1994, Byrd Cookie Company won the Fancy Food Small Packaging Award for its bold, innovative look.

Increased media exposure, including stories on CNN and in *Southern Living* and the *New York Times*, boosted sales substantially. In 1998, the company introduced a new line of jams, relishes, and condiments, aptly called Byrd Basics.

In May, 1995, Byrd Cookie Company moved into a modern, climate-controlled bakery. At 65,000 square feet, the plant was four times the size of the former facility! In addition, the retail store, now titled the Gourmet Marketplace, was enlarged to 2,400 square feet. In this new location, with beautiful and eclectic merchandise, sales have increased by 450 percent. With an eye always to the future, another look in packaging was designed in 1998. The colorful, creative look became an instant success. Praised for Best Cookie Packaging by *Food Distributions* Magazine in 1998, the company awaits even more accolades in the coming years.

What's in store for Byrd Cookie Company? Only the Curl family knows for sure. But as consumers continue to enjoy the tiny, delectable cookies created by a legacy, they all agree on one thing. Byrd Cookies are becoming more than just a satisfying treat. They're becoming a passion.

"Caught with his hand in the cookie jar again." Phillip Curl, fifth generation cookie baker.

Sarah Elizabeth Bradford

Enterprise Index

Gulfstream Aerospace Corporation
PO Box 2206
Savannah, Georgia 31402-2206
Phone: 912-965-3000
Fax: 912-965-3775
www.gulfstream.com
Pages 134-137

The Hilton Savannah DeSoto
15 East Liberty Street
Savannah, Georgia 31401
Phone: 912-232-9000
Fax: 912-231-1633
E-mail: nrackley@desotohilton.com
www.hilton.com
Pages 182-183

H.O. Systems
222 West Oglethorpe Avenue
Savannah, Georgia 31401
Phone: 912-527-4040
Fax: 912-527-4011
E-mail: hart.williford@hosystems.com
www.hosystems.com
Pages 126-129

Hunter, Maclean, Exley & Dunn, P.C.
200 East Saint Julian Street
Savannah, Georgia 31401
Phone: 912-236-0261
Fax: 912-234-9296
E-mail: ouidf@huntermaclean.com
www.huntermaclean.com
Page 158

InterMarine Savannah
301 North Lathrop
Savannah, Georgia 31415
Phone: 912-234-6579
Fax: 912-236-8887
E-mail: info@intermarinesavannah.com
www.intermarinesavannah.com
Pages 148-149

J.T. Turner Construction Co., Inc.
PO Box 10046
2250 East Victory Drive, Suite 104
Savannah, Georgia 31412
Phone: 912-356-5611
Fax: 912-356-5615
E-mail: mturner@jttconst.com
www.jttconst.com
Page 165

Memorial Health
4700 Waters Avenue
PO Box 23089
Savannah, Georgia 31404
Phone: 912-350-8000
www.memorialhealth.com
Page 172

Pitney Bowes
8001 Chatham Center Drive
Savannah, Georgia 31405
Phone: 912-644-6800
Fax: 912-644-6795
www.pb.com
Pages 156-157

Savannah Area Chamber of Commerce
101 East Bay Street
PO Box 1628
Savannah, Georgia 31401
Phone: 912-644-6400
Fax: 912-644-6498
E-mail: ebackus@savcvb.com
www.savannahchamber.com
Page 152-153

Savannah College of Art and Design
PO Box 3146
Savannah, Georgia 31402-3146
Phone: 800-869-SCAD
Fax: 912-525-5983
www.scad.edu
Pages 170-171

Savannah Technical College
5717 White Bluff Road
Savannah, Georgia 31405-5521
Phone: 912-351-6362
Fax: 912-303-1707
E-mail: dbrown@savtec.org
www.savannah.tec.ga.us
Pages 173

WSAV
1430 East Victory Drive
Savannah, Georgia 31404
Phone: 912-651-0300
Fax: 912-651-0320 (News)
E-mail: mail@wsav.com
www.wsav.com
Pages 130-131

Index